Mother
As Emotional Coach

8 Principles for Raising a Well-Adjusted Child

Stephany Hughes, PhD

outskirts press
DENVER, COLORADO

The opinions expressed in this manuscript are solely the opinions of the author and do not represent the opinions or thoughts of the publisher. The author has represented and warranted full ownership and/or legal right to publish all the materials in this book.

Mother As Emotional Coach:
8 Principles for Raising a Well-Adjusted Child
All Rights Reserved.
Copyright © 2015 Stephany Hughes, PhD
v4.0

Cover Photo © 2015 Getty Images.com. All rights reserved - used with permission.

This book may not be reproduced, transmitted, or stored in whole or in part by any means, including graphic, electronic, or mechanical without the express written consent of the publisher except in the case of brief quotations embodied in critical articles and reviews.

Outskirts Press, Inc.
http://www.outskirtspress.com

ISBN: 978-1-4787-3785-8

Library of Congress Control Number: 2014916077

Outskirts Press and the "OP" logo are trademarks belonging to Outskirts Press, Inc.

PRINTED IN THE UNITED STATES OF AMERICA

*In Memory of
Nona Tollefson
1937-2004
Mentor, Professor, Friend
University of Kansas*

Table of Contents

Endorsements vii
Preface ix
How You Might Use This Book xiii
Acknowledgments xv

<u>The Eight Principles</u>

Chapter 1: Principle One: Your children are watching you. 1
Chapter 2: Principle Two: Give devotion to your work. 8
Chapter 3: Principle Three: There are better smarts than book smarts .. 17
Chapter 4: Principle Four: Read, read, read, and then read some more . 26
Chapter 5: Principle Five: You must help your children quiet their minds, unclutter their lives, and cut down on their activities 32
Chapter 6: Principle Six: Intuition is your best teacher 38
Chapter 7: Principle Seven: Your child will thrive and develop a wider range of emotions if he feels your support and unconditional love. 48
Chapter 8: Principle Eight: You and your child can become empowered through praying. 56

<u>The Overexcitabilities</u>

Chapter 9: What's That Big Word and What Does It Have To Do With Me? 63
Chapter 10: Your Child Might Not Have ADHD (Attention Deficit with Hyperactivity Disorder) 66
Chapter 11: It's Your Fault The Kid's So Smart 70
Chapter 12: They're Not Wasting Time Playing Legos 74
Chapter 13: Secrets of a Drama Queen (and Why Being One is a Good Thing) 80
Chapter 14: Where's My Blankie? 85
Conclusion: You ARE an Emotional Coach 90
Appendix I: The Theory of Positive Disintegration 93
Appendix II: Developmental Potential 98
Appendix III: A Poem by Kazimierz Dabrowski 100
Bibliography 101

Endorsements

"Dr. Stephany Hughes has written one of the most practical, down-to-earth authoritative guides to parenting now available. If you treasure common sense and a mother's actual experience, expressed in plain language, you will love this book."

—Larry Dossey, MD
Author: *One Mind: How Our Individual Mind is Part of a Greater Consciousness and Why It Matters*

"I have always felt parents should have to earn a license before raising a family. Stephany's book can become the resource and guide to your obtaining that license and becoming your child's life coach."

—Bernie Siegel, MD
Author: *Love, Magic & Mudpies* and *Prescriptions for Living*

"This is one book this old clergyman wishes he had years ago when, together with his wife, was raising three children. It offers the wisdom of the ages with the smarts of today's brightest. With the help of this book, I could have been the father I yearned to be. This gem of a book combines the wisdom of writers of the past with the latest wisdom of the present. Read it now and avoid the regrets of the future."

—Dr. Robert H. Meneilly
Pastor Emeritus
Village United Presbyterian Church
Author: *Happiness, the Real Thing* and *Pray as You Go*

"In *Mother as Emotional Coach: Raising a Well-Adjusted Child*, Hughes lays a clear path through the tangled landscape of parenting. The Eight Principles outlined are practical and inspiring, a rare combination in parenting books, highlighting that, "the ultimate direction and control of behavior is located in the emotional rather than in the intellectual function." Hughes includes in her foundation many practical ideas to create a community for mothers. As the mother of three children and as an educator, I inhaled these ideas, informed by both compassion and sound pedagogy."

—Dawn Wink, M.A.
Author: *Teaching Passionately: What's Love Got To Do With It?*
and *Meadowlark*

Preface

"Society has much to gain from examining its most evolved members." It was a quotation on the cover of a new publication, <u>Journal of Advanced Development</u>. I was on my way to an educational convention where I would be running into the editor of the journal, and I wanted to read the articles in it before I saw her. Little did I know how much influence her journal would have on my life.

The first article in the journal, entitled, "Dabrowski's Theory of Positive Disintegration," was written by Karen C. Nelson. I had no idea what the theory was about, but I did wonder if the author was the same Karen Nelson I knew. Quickly thumbing to the article and reading the author's biography, I discovered she was who I thought she was, a professor at Emporia State University. I was now doubly delighted with the journal, because not only did my friend write the lead article, but I already knew the journal was edited by another colleague, Linda Krieger Silverman, founder of the Institute for the Study of Advanced Development, located in Denver, Colorado.

Arriving at the convention in Little Rock, Arkansas, the first person I saw was Linda Silverman. I congratulated her on her new journal and told her how much I liked it, enthusiastically explaining my reaction to Karen's article, and asked her to autograph the journal, which she happily did.

After autographing the cover, she turned to the inside and wrote, "Dear Stephany, Thank you for appreciating the theory and my new baby. Linda." Then she went on to tell me that I was the first person who had actually read the journal. She said most of her friends had congratulated her on publishing it, but none of them had read it yet.

As Linda and I discussed the article that had impacted me, I learned more about Kazimierz Dabrowski (1902-1980), a Polish psychiatrist and psychologist, who created and researched his Theory of Positive Disintegration as a result of his personal experiences, especially those involving death, suffering, the meaning of human existence and the destiny of humanity, in his adolescent years during World War II. He also drew heavily from his clinical practice as a psychotherapist, as well as from his study of gifted, creative and eminent individuals.

I told Linda that I had experienced an "A-ha!" moment, a personal epiphany, as I read the article. As I discovered the five levels of the theory, the five overexcitabilities, that are indicators of developmental potential and the implications of the theory for gifted individuals, it was as if I were reading about myself. It explained to me why, even though my IQ is probably not particularly high, I had probably used the five overexcitabilities in nurturing my own developmental potential.

Linda went on to explain that Dabrowski's theory, unlike most other psychologies of persons, does not interest itself in discovering a hypothetical "norm" or average of human behavior. Instead, in this theory, the ultimate direction and control of behavior is located in the *emotional* rather than in the *intellectual* function.

Immediately, from our discussion and from reading the article, I knew I wanted to use Dabrowski's Theory as the basis for my doctoral dissertation, and I knew who my participants would be. I had been attending several conventions and seminars around the country on the topic of spirituality. At these training sessions, I had listened to and interacted with speakers whose books I had read and whose writings had influenced my thinking and behavior.

These individuals lived an authentic life, and wrote books to share their life experiences with others. They had become eminent spiritual leaders, even though they had not started out with that end in mind.

If I could ascertain how these eminent individuals had managed to live up to their own ideals, their experiences and behaviors might inspire others who are challenged by events in their own lives. Somehow, others might feel their personal life experiences, even the painful ones, had a meaningful purpose, particularly those experiences involving parenthood.

Researching and writing my dissertation was life changing for me. It changed the way I looked at the world and the people in it. I interviewed the participants either by phone or in person. What each person shared about their life affected me as I swam in the data for months and months. The results and conclusions of my dissertation are the basis for this book.

When I finished my dissertation and graduated, I knew I wanted to write a book. I wanted to share what I had learned by distilling the conclusions into an easy-to-read guide that would help parents. I want parents to know that what they are going through is worth it—all the long hours, the discipline, the hanging in there and being present for their kids. All those sacrifices pale in comparison to the joy one feels when children turn out right.

The purpose of this book is to help you look at yourself and how you are conducting your life, so you can either congratulate yourself and affirm that you are doing an excellent job, or to admit to yourself that you might need to examine the model you are presenting for your child's future.

If parents can realize the importance of the eight principles presented here, take them to heart, apply them to their own lives, and therefore, become a model of emotional development for their children, parenthood can be more joyful and fulfilling. Children will have happier and more successful lives. I wish you the best as you embark on this journey for your children and for yourself.

How You Might Use This Book

As I wrote this book, I kept in mind my intended audience—mothers of young children; in particular, I kept in mind my daughter-in-law, Tanya Hughes. She is the stay-at-home mom of my three grandchildren, ages 11, 8 and 5. When we visit, I see how much of her time and energy she puts into parenting. I marvel also at how clean her house is, how nutritious the meals are, and how the laundry is always done.

Then I think, "Oh, I used to do that," and cannot believe I ever did. I'm also wondering how moms with all this responsibility will have time to read this book, but I look back and realize that no matter how precious my spare time was, I always found time to read. This is what I hope you are doing. Make time to read, no matter what.

Even if you did not have good parenting yourself, you can educate yourself by reading. This is very important to you and your child's development.

Then what? Here are some suggestions for how to get the most out of the ideas presented in this book:

At the end of each chapter, the main points are summarized and you will find a few quick exercises to do. These exercises will help you apply what you are learning to your parenting skills. I want you to be a parent who knows what you are doing and why. I want you to see behavioral results in yourself and in your children.

Create a parents' reading circle and meet regularly to discuss the concepts presented here. Do a chapter or two at a time then talk about insights, improvements and issues at your next meeting. Take turns being the facilitator.

Use this book as a basis for discussion at your religious education classes.

Write a class proposal for your local adult education bulletin, offering to facilitate it. Meet eight times or so, in the daytime or the evening.

If you are a writer, do morning pages for a few minutes each day for several weeks. Julia Cameron created the idea of morning pages and this has helped many people put their thoughts and feelings on paper, which can be very therapeutic and cathartic. Her website is artistsway.com.

Start a meet-up group (meetup.com or Google hangout). If you work outside the home during the day, perhaps this would be an easy method for meeting in the evening or on the weekend with like-minded people.

Start a blog. Ask others to follow it and to comment. Discuss the theories presented in the book, beginning with how they apply to you, then moving on to how you can use what you've learned to better understand your children.

Acknowledgments

I dedicate this book to the memory of Nona Tollefson, who guided me through my dissertation at the University of Kansas. Those of you lucky enough to have had her for a professor or advisor know how invaluable she was to the completion of your work. I feel blessed to have known her.

Then there are the women who edited my work. They are all gifted writers in their own right and it was my luck that placed them on my pathway. Carol Newman, you guided me through the first section; Deborah Shouse, we plowed through to the end, and Ashley Hughes, my daughter, you did a clean sweep through the whole book, then were invaluable down the home stretch to publication.

Doug, you are the best father our children could have imagined. You were always there for them, loving them, giving your all and making them your priority.

John, you were there for me at the end, working out all the technical glitches without a word of why couldn't I do that myself. I'm so lucky to have you.

Thanks to all of you. You helped make my dreams come true. It is said that 85% of the population wants to write a book, but only 5% actually do it, and I know why: they didn't have you helping them. It takes a very large village to write and publish a book.

I want to share what I discovered about emotional development while doing the research for my doctoral dissertation. I want mothers of young children to read it and know they are performing the most important job in the whole world. Thank you, mothers. You have my deepest admiration for the hard work you do every single day of your life.

CHAPTER 1

Principle One:
Your children are watching you.

Being a mother is the grandest calling a woman can have. Your children are your future. You want them to be successful. You want them to be well-behaved. You want them to be educated. You want them to be happy. This book will give you information to make you aware of how all of that hinges on your emotional development. You will learn ways to use your own intuition and intelligence, while raising children who have a strong sense of self and consideration for others.

In later chapters, I'm going to tell you about a theory developed by a man who can help you understand yourself better, Dr. Kamierz Dabrowski, a psychiatrist who did research on emotional development in Poland during World War II. In his theory, there are five levels of emotional development and five "overexciteabilities" which help individuals move through the levels.

You are a powerful influence on your child.

Children go through their developmental stages quickly. You only have a short time to influence them. It is said that a child's values and foundation for life are formed by age six. That means everything you do, every word you say, each experience you have together, is meaningful.

◄ MOTHER AS EMOTIONAL COACH

Imagine yourself 25 years from now. Your children are grown and educated, perhaps married with children of their own. How you raised your children will influence every interaction you have with them and your grandchildren. I bet you want every family gathering or phone call to be enjoyable. I wager you want fun happening for every family member.

But wait! How about the now? What about the fact that you are exhausted much of the time, frustrated with your parenting skills, and don't seem to have a moment to call your own? All you want to do is go in your bedroom, close the door, and have a few moments to yourself, without some kid banging on the door and yelling for you at the top of his lungs.

Let life happen.

Letting life happen is difficult for mothers. We are accustomed to being in charge of our lives. We are comfortable being a take-charge kind of person in the work world. We were born to bring order out of chaos. We think we can do it all, have it all. Then reality hits. Our children are born and they have their own time schedules. As months go by and they are able to walk and talk, we come to the sudden realization that they have their own agenda and it's usually not what we have jotted down in our planners.

Suddenly, on a date somewhere around her second birthday, you and your child become locked into a "who's in charge here?" skirmish. It doesn't go away. It's here to stay. Who will win this battle of wills? Naturally, you're the bigger one, so logically, you should be the one winning. But you are frustrated. It seems like you're always in conflict about the tiniest things. Stop! Give up! You're not in charge. Sure, allow her choices about which outfit to wear, which vegetable to eat, and which game she wants to play. But, completely give up on controlling her personality traits, whether she is an introvert or extrovert, or how she reacts emotionally to situations. These things are pre-determined. You have nothing to do with them. You were the vessel she passed through on her way to her own destiny.

Each child is born with her own agenda, her separate DNA. She may look like you or her father, but sometimes that's where similarities end.

She's a complete entity unto herself. No other person has ever been like her, and it's your job to guide, discipline, and facilitate her as she develops. That is an honor and a privilege higher than any other you will ever receive. Oh, yes, and you get to pay for all of it, too.

Clashing is normal.

If you think you are the only mother who has conflict with your child and that you must be the meanest mother in the universe, think again. Conflict comes with the territory. The child I fought with for the first twelve years of his life could not be more unlike me. We don't have any of the same interests. He is content to be by himself; I am an extravert. He enjoys learning by himself; I like interacting with others to learn. He reads fantasy; I enjoy non-fiction. Our list of dissimilarities is endless. I wondered if we would ever make it through his growing-up years.

Today, at age forty-seven, he is one of my dearest friends and supporters. We know our differences and respect them. We marvel in disbelief at how each of us approaches life. But the bottom line for me is that he is a wonderful husband, a fabulous father, and an all-around great guy. I admire his ethics, values, and morals, plus he treats his mother (me) like a queen. So, you tell me—were all the nights my husband and I lay in bed worrying about him and all the fights we had worth it?

Accept the gift you've been given.

Your child is a gift, like no other, and you wouldn't want it any other way. Yet, *Your* "self" collides with *Her* "self" on a daily basis. We think it would be nice to have the perfect little family all standing neatly in a row, well-behaved, with their shirts unwrinkled, and no dirt on their faces. That is our fantasy. But let's face it—those ideal families don't exist. They look good on the pages of your favorite magazine, but life could get boring when you live in a model home with an exemplary family, where nothing ever goes wrong, the children are perpetually well-mannered, and you—well, you have made all of this happen with no muss nor fuss. All of this

MOTHER AS EMOTIONAL COACH

perfection is fun to dream about, but the real fun of parenting is discovering which shoe is going to fall first and what you're going to do about it when it does.

Love your child. Let her life take its own direction. Stop thinking she's going to play the violin when all she wants to do is beat out rhythms on her brother's drum set. Stop believing he is going to be super-stud athlete when what warms his heart is painting, nature, and animals.

Some of the most fun I've had with my own kids is watching them follow their own schemes. For example, when my daughter, Ashley, was in sixth grade, she suddenly had an urge to play the bagpipes. Where this urge originated, I didn't know, but I did know that finding bagpipe lessons was not going to be easy. With a little sleuthing, I found there was a bagpipe group in the city, so off we went. Unlike the flute, saxophone, and trumpet we had already purchased for her (and her two brothers') musical careers, a practice instrument was provided for her to play. We drove to the lessons for several months.

This whole bagpipe thing was beginning to scare me, as I began to imagine the purchase of an expensive instrument, concocting some sort of a bagpipe costume, then traveling to faraway states and even foreign countries to attend her bagpipe concerts. Luckily, after less than a year, Ashley lost interest.

Yet, had we not pursued her dream, we wouldn't have experienced the cultural and musical knowledge our entire family gained from it. Each week it had been an adventure, arising at an ungodly hour on Saturday morning and driving to a part of town where her father grew up, sitting there in the narthex of the Episcopal Church with our coffee, donuts, and the newspaper, trying to entertain ourselves while she rehearsed with the group. With each bite of donut, the bagpipe wailing became more and more forlorn. We rolled our eyes and went back to the sports page.

It's all worth it.

These and many other wild hares were followed by our family over the years. All of them were fun and all of them were quite a bit of trouble. We could have just as easily not done them, but I'm glad we did, because here are a few things I've noticed about these kids, now all grown:

They go out of their way for others. They love their relatives and love being with them, even if it means flying halfway across the country for an impromptu family gathering. Family, both extended and immediate, is their priority. They were watching us as we parented them. They noticed what kind of people we are, how we like to help others, and how our family made a special effort to be with the extended family on a regular basis.

I've noticed how they treat their own children and pets. They love the dickens out of them, yet have high standards for their behavior. They're passing it on.

Yes, your children are watching you. They notice how you recognize and honor each child's uniqueness, and how you allow them to follow their wildest dream, even for a short period of time until they get tired of it. All the while you are allowing life to flow, your children are flowing toward their own destinies. We, as parents, have no idea what those destinies are. All we have to do is allow our children to follow them, driving the tires off several vehicles in the process.

In the next chapter, you'll learn more about the flow of life and why it's good to go along with it.

Summary:
    A child is watching your every move.
    You are the greatest influence in your child's life.
    Don't fool yourself into thinking you are in charge.
    Conflict will occur.
    The greatest gift you'll ever receive is your child.
    Follow your child's whims.

MOTHER AS EMOTIONAL COACH

Something to think about:
1. Look at each of your children. Notice what they gravitate toward. Make a list of each child's talents.
2. Appreciate and point these out to your son or daughter as you observe them.
3. Be grateful for their marvelous diversity and unique personalities.
4. Do this even when they are hitting one another. Try not to swear at them.

Here is a poem that illustrates what I've been talking about:

You Thought I Wasn't Looking

When you thought I wasn't looking
You hung my first painting on the refrigerator
And I wanted to paint another.

When you thought I wasn't looking
You fed a stray cat.
And I thought it was good to be kind to animals.

When you thought I wasn't looking
You baked a birthday cake just for me
And I knew that little things were special things.

When you thought I wasn't looking
You said a prayer
And I believed there was a God that I could always talk to.

When you thought I wasn't looking
You kissed me good night

YOUR CHILDREN ARE WATCHING YOU

And I felt loved.

When you thought I wasn't looking
I saw tears come from your eyes
And I learned that sometimes things hurt, but that it's alright to cry.

When you thought I wasn't looking
You smiled
And it made me want to look that pretty, too.

When you thought I wasn't looking
You cared
And I wanted to be everything I could be.

When you thought I wasn't looking —
I looked—
And wanted to say "thanks" for all those things you did,

When you thought I wasn't looking.

—Mary Rita Schilke Korzan
Copyright 1980

CHAPTER **2**

Principle Two: Give devotion to your work.

Since your children are watching you, let's give them something worthwhile to watch. One of the best ways for you to be watched is while doing service for others. When you devote yourself to a worthy cause, your life will go in surprising directions. Helping others is one of the best ways to get your mind off yourself and your own situation.

So many times, we look at the problems in our own lives and we over-analyze them. We are so close to the situation, we don't see the big picture of how lucky we are and we overlook the abundance in our life. Sometimes we feel the need to acccumulate more possessions, both for ourselves and for our children. This turns into a vicious circle of consumption and we long to get out of it.

The solution is to get outside of our own milieu and into a different set of circumstances to learn gratitude and empathy. When we see the struggles of others and how they are coping, it makes us humble toward our own situation. Being of service also sends a strong message to your children.

Money isn't the issue.

Devotion to some type of work is critical to your emotional development. Devotion for work done today fires your furnace for tomorrow. It doesn't matter if your work is paid or volunteer. It's what gets you up in the morning, keeps your mind focused, and helps you be happily occupied for

GIVE DEVOTION TO YOUR WORK

a good portion of the day. You can't wait to see what will happen next on the project or creative work you are enjoying.

If you are devoted to your work, huge productivity and success are more likely. Likewise, your being happy in your life's work is critical to your child's emotional development. Your motivation and dedication to your work is what sets you apart. Your children can see you are deriving happiness through your work and they want what you have. They want to emulate you. You are their role model. You become an icon without having tried nor intended to.

Dabrowski's Theory of Emotional Development

In Chapter One, I told you about Dr. Kamierz Dabrowski who did research on emotional development. The person I have just described above has reached Level IV in Dabrowski's Theory of Emotional Development (See Appendix I for all five levels).

A person on level IV has found a way to meet her own ideals and she is an effective leader in society. This happens only if you are willing to transform yourself from "what is" to "what ought to be" because you have told yourself, "What ought to be, will be!" You are now demonstrating high levels of responsibility, authenticity, reflective judgment, empathy for others, autonomy of thought and action, and self-awareness.

Don't think your children aren't noticing this transformation and are internalizing it. They want to be like you, and what they see is who they aspire to be. Of course, they are at lower levels of emotional development than you are, but they see what they can become. This helps them advance in their own development at their own rate in their own time.

Things begin happening.

Eventually, your work of today somehow evolves into your work of tomorrow. It's an assignment, opportunity, or promotion you could never have imagined before—before you decided to start living the life that makes you happier and more fulfilled than you hardly think you deserve.

MOTHER AS EMOTIONAL COACH

You feel like an imposter. You feel lucky, although you know you jumped off an unknown cliff to get here. You're beginning to wonder if this is someone else's life.

Soon, your life has taken root and you start believing it's you who's living it. You love it, you deserve it, and by golly, you're going to keep advancing down this path because you can't wait to see what amazing thing is going to happen next.

And guess who's still watching you?

Stages of emotional development in children

A child begins at Level I in emotional development. This level is characterized by prevailing egocentrism. This is fine for a child because it's the way he's supposed to be at this stage of life. He wants what he wants when he wants it. You know what I mean. You see your child acting this way on a daily basis.

When things go wrong, someone else is always to blame. You've heard this dozens of times. It's always the other kid's fault. Self-responsibility is not a Level I characteristic. That's why they have you, teaching them to pick up their toys, brush their teeth, say "please" and "thank you," and an almost endless list of other things mothers do to tame their wild one into someone who demonstrates responsible human behavior. It isn't easy, but remember—it's worth it.

Without you there to inhibit their limitless personal ambition, Level I children grow up to become adults who often attain power in society by ruthless means. That's one big reason why your children need you as a mother. You are there to prevent this from happening.

Closing the door on your past

If you are a mother who was not well-parented, your heritage is not your fault. But how your children are parented as they grow up is your responsibility. If you have been abused or mistreated in some way, if your mother was unavailable because of alcohol or drug use, if you were neglected because of your father's gambling or absence, this has harmed your emotional development.

Please don't let your past keep you from soaring toward your own personal adult maturity. Do whatever it takes to courageously close that chapter of your life. There are support groups for practically every need these days. Don't be afraid to face your past. It might be difficult, but remember—your children are worth it, and so are you.

When parenting isn't positive

In my personal experience, I grew up with a nuclear family—mother, father, three brothers, and me. We lived in a small town in western Kansas where my father had his own business, and my mother was a homemaker. We went to church on Sunday, and lived a middle-class life with few bumps in the road. When I was eleven, my mother died of heart disease, leaving my father with four children ages 19, 16, 11, and 8 to raise by himself. That was the beginning of a different life for all of us.

My grandmother came frequently to help with the cooking, cleaning, and laundry. Our neighbors were generous to help out, especially the ones who took turns braiding my hair each day.

Back in the 50's, we didn't have grief counseling, or anything resembling that. We just sucked it up and went on the best we could.

As I look back, I can see my own emotional development was thwarted by my mother's absence. A girl needs her mother for many things and on many occasions. I was used to a mother who was always there for me. She was always there for my dance recitals. She worked hours on my costumes and I loved it when she finished one. I tried it on and felt like a show-girl. I loved tap-dancing and was accomplished at it. She and my father were my faithful audience and supporters.

She was always there for my birthdays, making sure I had a party, cake, and a cute new dress to wear. Even though I was a tomboy, she made certain my hair was feminine. Without her, I had to do everything for myself

MOTHER AS EMOTIONAL COACH

and I don't know that I always did a good job of it. I was too young. I was going through too many changes in my life to handle it alone.

In addition, I was thrust into her role in our household. I can tell you from my own experience that an eleven-year-old is too young to be given the day-to-day duties of keeping a house clean, cooking meals, and feeling responsible for a younger sibling.

In a couple of years, my dad remarried and I got the dreaded step-mother. She seemed to like my brothers okay, but when it came to me, she thought she had just inherited a Cinderella to do work around the house. I, of course, rebelled. I wasn't accustomed to a stranger telling me to hang the clothes on the line, to polish the silver, and to do the dishes (by hand). She was the general barking out orders and I was the private, bound and determined not to follow them.

Things went from bad to worse with our relationship, until one day I came home from seventh grade and she told me I didn't live there anymore. While I was at school, she had taken all of my belongings to my married brother's house, and now she was taking me there to live.

Years later, my sister-in-law told me that I didn't speak for two weeks. I have blocked that time out of my memory. I don't know what I was thinking or feeling at the time, but I imagine I was in shock. It was a long time until I would talk freely about it. I felt ashamed and embarrassed. I was rejected and abandoned.

I told you this story to illustrate that children can stop developing emotionally, and adults in their life usually have something to do with it. When I had my own children, I vowed two things to myself: I would not die while they were growing up, and my children would never have a step-mother. I would do everything in my power to follow a healthy lifestyle so I would be alive until they were grown, and no matter what, I would stay married while they were still dependent on their father and me. I kept those vows.

Reconciling what happened to me at the hands of my step-mother was a difficult task for me. It took close to twenty years, but I was determined that I would not let what happened to me affect my children. I read every parenting book available. I went to parenting seminars. I wanted to find out how to do the job right.

This is what I mean by gently closing the door of your past behind you. Everyone has some experience they need to lay to rest, and we can't move forward in a positive manner until we've done that difficult emotional work. I'm not saying it's easy and I'm not telling you it's quick. Just remember—it's worth it.

Some important work

After my children were grown, educated, and living independently, I looked forward to doing some volunteer work in other parts of the world. My husband and I had divorced and I was re-assessing my life and my priorities. I knew I wanted to live a life of service and I was exploring several options.

It took courage for me to choose to do a project for an organization called Global Volunteers. I frequently received brochures from this organization. It was summertime, and being a teacher, I had time available. This was an opportunity for me to branch out from my former married status. I examined the brochure for the myriad of places to go in the world. It scared me to break out that far, so I concentrated on opportunities in the United States.

I had been studying Kohlberg's Theory of Moral Development and Dabrowski's Theory of Emotional Development in my doctoral studies. The ideas in these theories nagged at me. If I ever wanted to advance my moral or emotional development, I needed to put myself in a place that would nudge me into reality, somewhere unlike my comfortable suburban lifestyle.

Evaluating myself to be opposite on the moral and emotional scale from Mother Teresa, I wanted to start inching my way up. I wanted to discover what it would be like to help others on their home turf. The whole idea filled me with fear of the unknown. That meant I had to go. My

MOTHER AS EMOTIONAL COACH

favorite quote says, "You must do the thing you think you cannot do," by Eleanor Roosevelt.

I chose a project to help create a summer day camp in Jonestown, Mississippi. Volunteers from all over the country would come together in Jonestown, create a program on the spot with a minimal amount of supplies and materials, then go to the community center and implement it with local kids.

As I read about the locale, "the poorest town in the poorest county in the United States," I knew I was in for a unique experience. I had no idea what it would be like, and if I had known ahead of time, I probably wouldn't have gone.

The volunteers had been instructed to meet at the Memphis, Tennessee, airport on that muggy summer day. There were 18 of us, ranging in age from teenagers to retirees, with equal numbers of men and women. We were greeted at the baggage claim area by several members of the community, who drove us to Jonestown, a little more than an hour south of Memphis.

Jonestown was a dusty little town of 1,200 residents. Along the dirt streets were neighborhoods of dilapidated houses. It was August, the temperature was 103 degrees, and I was in for the shock of my life.

Most of the volunteers stayed at the large, air-conditioned convent, but I was assigned to stay in a private home. As the car stopped in front of the McKnight family home, I braced myself. The one-story, unpainted wooden structure had a concrete porch with two leaning steps leading up to it. This is where I would stay for eight days. What had I done to myself?

Inside, there were two bedrooms, one bathroom, a kitchen, and a living area. As I glanced out the back door, I noticed standing water in the yard, which I later learned was their sewer water. My hostess, Gloria, was friendly. She appeared to be around forty, slender, well-dressed, and pretty. She introduced me to her children: General, 14; Devante, 10; and Jeremy, 8. A daughter and her baby also lived there and would be home later. No father was in the home.

GIVE DEVOTION TO YOUR WORK

Gloria gave me one of the bedrooms and said to make myself comfortable, but this was difficult to do because there was no air-conditioning. If it the temperature was 103 degrees, outside, heaven only knows how hot it was inside the house. Gloria walked down to a neighbor's house and returned with a fan, which she sat on a chair. She aimed the blast of hot air at my bed, and told me not to open the windows because there were no screens and the bugs would come in.

It was getting dark and the temperature was down into the mid-90's. I couldn't stay in the house. I was suffocating. I decided to go sit on the porch to cool off.

Soon, I wasn't sitting by myself. Several kids and teen-agers from the neighborhood noticed me and decided to come introduce themselves. One by one, they asked if they could join me. I was happy to have the company.

I noticed the quart bottle of beer one of the young men was drinking. Suddenly, I realized how I was going to sleep in the hot house! I would drink myself silly so I wouldn't notice I was sleeping in downtown Hades.

After inquiring where he got the beer, I asked him if he would go get me a bottle and to get everyone else on the porch a soda. I gave him twenty dollars, and he soon returned with our beverages. Soon, we were having the best time sitting and visiting on the front porch of the friendliest house in Jonestown.

Little did I know when I finally crawled into bed that night that I was about to experience what it was like to live at the survival level. I would learn how to live in the NOW and to be content with what I had. That night was a turning point in my life and I didn't even know it.

All the time I was in Jonestown, my children were watching me from afar, thinking I was nuts for being there, but nonetheless, still watching me.

Summary:

Work, paid or volunteer, is important for your emotional development.

◄ MOTHER AS EMOTIONAL COACH

You are responsible for your child's early emotional development. Do what it takes to resolve your past hurts.
Something to think about:

1. Think about the work you are doing. Evaluate its value to your emotional development. Think about the steps you could take to make your career dreams come true.

2. Think about what unfinished business you have from your past. Investigate what help you could get to resolve it.

CHAPTER 3

Principle Three: There are better smarts than book smarts.

You are a mother whose children are still in their crucial developmental stages. You are probably a mother who is book smart. You've educated yourself, probably at the collegiate level. You are seeking the best knowledge you can find through reading parenting books, taking continuing education classes, and consulting with both older and contemporary mothers. You've realized your children aren't perfect, and neither are you. The most important piece of information you can learn is this: how much you know isn't nearly as important as how much you love.

The tools are here to help you raise and love your children, plus some ideas to challenge your thinking about your priorities. Who you are—you as a person—is the most important element in your child's growth and development. It's who you are, not the number of play groups and sports activities your child participates in, that will determine how he moves through the stages of emotional development.

As for you, the parent, who you are was determined by your parents in your early developmental stages, but as you entered your schooling phase, suddenly there were a myriad of other individuals who were influencing you. You were at Level II in emotional development, where you did what

MOTHER AS EMOTIONAL COACH

other people told you to do. You didn't have your own rules. When you were a child at Level II, you thought rules were external and it was your job to follow them. Sometimes you took a risk and broke the rules, but there were still rules set before you.

This is why it is important for you to have rules for your children. Rules are the benchmark by which they regulate their own behavior, and when they stray from the mark, it is your duty as a parent to correct their course. This isn't easy. It means sticking with them, making sure they know you are watching. It means giving directions and expecting they will be followed. It means having consistent rules for discipline and enforcing them. You must keep your children inside your behavioral boundaries because they don't have personal boundaries yet. It means giving up some of your pleasure and leisure so you can be alert to what your children are doing and saying. Watching happens both ways!

Parents I watched following these guidelines while visiting in our home were my niece, Shelly, and her husband, Ladd. They had two small children, Natalie, age 7, and Austin, age 3. We were happy to have them visit because we knew Shelly and Ladd were always aware of where the children were and what they were doing. Neither parent was hesitant to discipline the kids in front of us. If Natalie got sassy, even just a little bit, she was instantly reminded of her behavior and was informed to stop that kind of talk. If Austin got a bit too rambunctious in the house, he was reminded to stop and pay attention to what he was doing.

The youngsters had boundaries and rules, and were reminded of them on a consistent basis. If they disobeyed or stepped outside their behavioral limits after the first reminder, one or the other parent took them for a "bedroom chat," followed by a time-out. I don't know what they said to the kids in their chat room, but it was effective, because the children stopped doing what they had been chided for when they returned. It was a pleasure to observe their active parenting.

THERE ARE BETTER SMARTS THAN BOOK SMARTS

Today, those children are 30 and 26. They are well-mannered, polite, and highly regarded by everyone in our family as well as by others they meet. It wasn't easy for Shelly and Ladd at the time, but now they are reaping the rewards from having applied discipline in their children's lives at an early age. They have offspring who are a pleasure to be around, who achieved in school, and are on their way to a great future.

Having boundaries, rules, and discipline means you won't always be popular with your children. They may dislike you some of the time, and your feelings mirror their feelings, more than you want to admit. In fact, many times you might wonder why you ever had them in the first place. You didn't know being a parent was going to be this difficult. Well, it is, and you are going to stay the course, because remember—*it's worth it.*

Your child's progression through the levels of emotional development is influenced more by significant people than by academic achievement. Some of those significant people might be teachers. Others could be coaches or Scout leaders. One might be a neighbor who is supportive of your child.

For me, one such person was Aunt Sarah. Although she wasn't my aunt, she was our neighbor across the street. She was an older woman who had raised one son. She reveled in telling me and my brothers how wonderful we were. She baked cookies for us. She came to our performances. She supported us in every way one human could support another.

Another one of my significant role models was my Latin teacher, Ruth Darst. She was stringent with her students, demanded the best from us, and we rose to the occasion every time. I use what she taught me every day of my life, not only the academics, but also the personal characteristics of perseverance, excellence, and courage. She taught me the value of discipline. Every day we had an assignment and I knew I must have it done by the next day, or I would incur the wrath of Ruth. I also knew the assignment had better be correct. She set high standards and I wanted to meet them.

MOTHER AS EMOTIONAL COACH

In college, Professor Morrill, my English teacher, encouraged me. He let me know, with the class listening, that I was a good writer and had something worthwhile to say. I'll always remember the day he allowed me to read what I had written as a good example of the assignment he had given.

My friend's mother, Mona, taught me to always look my best when going out in public. Her daughter, Suzanne, and I, laughed about our in-house fashion guide, but to this day, I thank her for giving us rules to follow. When she died at 93, I jokingly asked if it would please her if we wore white gloves, hats, and pantyhose to her funeral.

Without these people, and many more who encouraged me, I would have wandered through my developmental years, wondering if I was doing things correctly. With them, however, I had guideposts marking every step of the way. They led me through my growing-up years, giving me models to emulate and ideals to live up to.

Level II behavior in your child.

Children at Level II are influenced mainly by their social group and by mainstream values. They often seem indecisive and ambivalent about how they feel because they have no clear-cut set of self-determined values. Values are internalized from external sources. To a child, opposing choices have equal value. The choices they make are for the most part determined by the moment and the circumstance. They have simultaneous feelings, such as like/dislike, approach/avoidance, inferiority/superiority, and love/hate.

I'll bet you've also noticed mood fluctuations in your child, sometimes alternating between excitement and inhibition. You might also notice indecision, wanting and not wanting, wanting two irreconcilable things at once, and having self-defeating behaviors.

You probably realize this description is hitting pretty close to home. It describes your child's behavior on many days. Take courage in the fact that

THERE ARE BETTER SMARTS THAN BOOK SMARTS

it's normal behavior. On Levels I and II, the personality ideal is an imitation. Children want to emulate their heroes in sports, movies, or magazines.

Important role models

When I was growing up, mothers were at home. When my brothers and I raced into the house after school, there she was, waiting for us and any friends we may have brought along. Our Brownie leader was my mother's friend. Our church choir director was my teacher. Our church school teacher was a neighbor down the street. Everywhere I went, someone knew me and was watching out for me, as well as watching me, and I knew it.

I wasn't allowed to go to the movies because my grandparents were Quakers and they didn't believe in the influence of media. The only magazines I saw were *Highlights for Children*, *Girl Scout Journal*, and *Wee Wisdom*. The most risque' photos I saw were a few bare-breasted African women in *National Geographic*. We didn't have television, and my winter evenings were filled with reading *Nancy Drew*, *The Hardy Boys*, and *Cherry Ames, Student Nurse*. In the summer, neighborhood kids and I stayed out until after dark playing softball, kick the can, or hide and seek. Life was innocent and children felt safe.

With my own children, we had television—*Happy Days*, *Emergency with Roy and Johnny*, and *The Brady Bunch*. We had soccer, piano lessons, and Scouts. Again, simple and innocent.

I don't envy you mothers today who have to cope with day care, the internet and cable TV. Your job is much more difficult. Keeping track of your kids and what they're doing is no easy task. Even though you don't allow certain things at your home, perhaps some of the homes have more relaxed rules where your children visit. You need to get some significant role models in your child's life, but you need to know them. Participate in your child's activities and know the people to whom you entrust your child.

Not all adults are trustworthy. We have learned that trusting your clergy can be iffy. Your coach's motives might be in question. You almost

MOTHER AS EMOTIONAL COACH

feel the need to run an FBI check on your day care provider or your child's Scout leader.

Teach your children it is okay to not be nice when it comes to their personal safety. They need to know when their personal boundaries are being invaded and that it's okay to report adults who are trying to overstep their authority. Remember, your child's personality ideal at this stage is imitation, so give them some positive role models to imitate.

Day camp in Jonestown

In Jonestown, one of our jobs was to be a positive role model the children might be lacking in their lives, because so few of the children knew their fathers, and their mothers were absent for much of the day.

Monday morning dawned in Jonestown with the rooster's crow. Gloria got up early and went to work at 7:30. I got up a little bit later and decided to help the McKnight kids get organized for the day. DeVante and Jeremy were going to the day camp, and I asked what they were going to wear. They went to the closet and opened the door. There on the floor was a pile containing everyone's clothes. They each grabbed an outfit.

I noticed the outfits needed ironing, so Jeremy, the second grader, plugged in the iron and using the bed for a board, he ironed his shirt and shorts. DeVante put his clothes on without ironing them. They weren't having any breakfast, so I couldn't help them with that.

I needed to leave an hour before camp started so I could go to the convent for breakfast, participate in our morning meditation, then walk over to the community center and get set up. I waved good-bye to the boys and said I'd see them soon.

What we wanted to accomplish

Our volunteer group had spent all afternoon and evening the day before creating a five-day curriculum for the day camp. First, we set our goals for the week: Joy, Team, Learn, and Serve. We wanted to have fun

THERE ARE BETTER SMARTS THAN BOOK SMARTS

with the children, within the team, and with members of the community. We wanted to experience some rare moments of joy—moments that fill your heart. Making new friends was important, while being an effective team of competent individuals. All of us had come to immerse ourselves in an ethnic culture, while learning about local history. Each of us thought we would gain self-knowledge from the experience.

Finally, we wanted to touch lives. We wanted to do our part to improve race relations, just by being there. We wanted to do what the community had requested of us—facilitate a summer learning experience for their children.

We planned games, both for inside and outside the community center. Some volunteers wanted to do puzzles with the children. Others wanted to do crafts. One young man could play the guitar, so we prepared a few songs to get us started. The day camp was to run from nine until noon. Each afternoon, we planned to eat lunch together at the convent, then spend a couple of hours processing the morning and planning for the next day.

The community center was a new, yet plain rectangle building surrounded by a patch of grass. It was painted white and had many windows. Our first job was to raise all the windows, because we knew it would soon be sweltering inside if we didn't. There was no running water, so we hauled coolers of water and ice from the convent, plus provided a cup with each child's name on it. We efficiently went about setting up the different activity stations.

Soon, it was nine, but only DeVante and Jeremy had arrived. I soon learned there had been no advance publicity for the day camp. No wonder we had no campers. They didn't know about it. Taking Jeremy with me, I set out to recruit potential campers from the neighborhood. He showed me where a few of his friends lived in apartments across the street. We were able to find several boys and girls to come to the community center and see what we were offering.

After about an hour of walking around the various neighborhoods, we were relieved to see boys and girls trickling into the community center.

MOTHER AS EMOTIONAL COACH

Word travels fast in a small town, and soon the center was filled with happy, giggling children, eager to participate in the activities we had prepared for them.

Loving the kids

The children were endearing. We bonded with them immediately. I was touched emotionally by them. Several times during the morning, I felt like crying. They were engaged and learning, plus I could see they were having fun. There was no time to dwell on my emotions, though, as Ebony needed some glue for her purple tissue-paper dinosaur, DeVante wanted a drink, Chantelle asked me if I liked her painting, and Markevious ran around painting his face while rummaging through the art supplies.

At noon, the other volunteers and I offered the children popcorn to take with them as they left, not knowing if they would get anything else for lunch. We were exhausted. Rivulets of perspiration poured down my face. I did have something to anticipate for the afternoon, however. The manager of the Comfort Inn in Clarksdale, a town fifteen miles away, invited the volunteers to use their swimming pool each afternoon. As I rushed to eat lunch so we could go swim, I didn't realize that another feeling was about to overtake me—guilt.

Summary:

Set firm rules for your children and enforce them.

Parenting is not a popularity contest.

How much you know isn't nearly as important as how much you love.

Role models play a significant part in your child's emotional development.

Have fun with your kids.

THERE ARE BETTER SMARTS THAN BOOK SMARTS

Something to think about:

1. Think back to your own childhood and formative years. Recall the individuals who made a big difference in your life. Reflect on how that helped shape who you are today. Tell your children about these significant individuals so they can be aware of the people in their lives who are making a difference.

2. Ask your children about their own personal triumphs and accomplishments, then have them name those individuals who helped them with their achievements.

3. If your children get a few lower grades than you expected, examine your reactions to their less-than-perfect selves. Don't lock them in their room until they raise their grades. They'll remember that for a long time, but not in a good way.

CHAPTER 4

Principle Four: Read, read, read, and then read some more

According to Kamierz Dabrowski's Theory of Positive Disintegration, a fancy name for his Theory of Emotional Development (don't even try to remember those words, but I'll tell you later about the disintegration part), if you expect your children to attain higher levels of emotional development, you must see to it that they go beyond Level I, where they lack empathy and self-examination. You must also help them go higher than Level II, where the child is influenced primarily by their social group and mainstream values.

Your job as a parent is to boost them into Level III, where a youngster must be able to assert self-awareness, self-direction, and self-discipline. As you look at your child today, these descriptors might seem a far reach from her present behavior. But hold on. Don't give up. This is the stage where she needs you the most.

If you can guide your child to Level III, she will find herself in the position where she can envision the way she would like to be. However, she does not yet hold the means of meeting her own ideals. That is where reading comes in. What she reads is extremely valuable to her. All kids need lots of time to read good literature and need to be given additional

READ, READ, READ, AND THEN READ SOME MORE

time with you or other significant adults to process their reading experiences. You need to be there so they can talk about the inner conflicts they encounter in their reading. They need to be able to contrast the "what is" in their world with the vision of "what ought to be" as they read.

Time spent with authors and their writing, in addition to time spent with you to process his feelings, gives your child the opportunity to have outward expression of the moral dilemmas he reads about. He needs to be given a chance to discuss these feelings.

You are at a higher level than your youngster who is feeling inner conflicts; therefore, you can present a point of view previously unconsidered by him. Teachers, mentors, peers, and parents need to listen to children's wonderings about the meaning of life, for it is through this questioning of "what is" that children begin to psychically disintegrate (there's that word!) the societal norms within them. They begin to experience the great joy that comes from being aware of their own uniqueness.

To psychically disintegrate means to discard one's previous way of thinking and to begin allowing new ways of thinking to enter our being. For example, your child might be afraid of police officers. Then one day, a police officer comes to his school and talks to his class, or finds his lost puppy, or helps his grandmother when she called 911. Suddenly, your child sees a police officer who is kind and helpful, and replaces his original concept of police officers with a new perception.

In his process of questioning what he sees in the world compared to what he is feeling inside, the simpler and less mature psychological structures (remember Levels I and II?) break down in order for more complex and advanced structures to arise. These structures are found at Levels III, IV, and V. Another fact you need to know about disintegration is when you leave a level behind, you never return to that level's behavior without knowing it is wrong. Previous structures psychically disintegrate. Think of it as growing up or maturing.

MOTHER AS EMOTIONAL COACH

It is at Level III that individuals are able to use their self-awareness, self-direction, and self-discipline to overcome genetic tendencies, less-than-optimal upbringing, and external circumstances beyond their control. Now you can see how, if a youngster's development is arrested at Level II, there is little chance of him being able to assess his talents and to develop them. He doesn't have the tools and skills necessary to advance. It's not his fault. One of the ways for him to disintegrate his lower-level structures is by reading. I think that's what I did.

Reading played a huge role in my development. I don't remember learning to read or being taught to read. I know I could read in the first grade, because I remember thinking how silly it was to read, "Run, Spot, Run." I couldn't figure out why the same words were repeated over and over. Instead of reading or learning, I spent first grade working puzzles at the play table or being the class librarian.

My parents read to me regularly. I loved hearing fairy tales, such as *Snow White and the Seven Dwarfs* and *Cinderella*. My imagination went wild as I heard it read aloud while looking at the pictures.

My favorite was *The Princess and the Pea*. I identified greatly with this story. Every night after I heard the story, I imagined there was a lump in my mattress caused by a pea. I thought myself a Princess.

In second grade, I raced through *The Bobbsey Twins* series. I loved those books. They may have prepared me for becoming a mother of boy-girl twins later on. The next series I tackled was *The Hardy Boys*. I loved their adventures and their rough-and-tumble ways. They reminded me of my brothers and all the trouble they were constantly getting themselves into.

Since I was in a family of boys, I read all the series about basketball and baseball characters. They were written in formula style. Each new one was identical to the one I had just read, but they were page-turners. I stayed up late at night with a flashlight under the covers reading until the exciting ending of the championship game.

READ, READ, READ, AND THEN READ SOME MORE

Then there was the *Cherry Ames, Student Nurse* series. I didn't particularly like these books, but all my friends were reading them, so I followed the crowd (typical Level II behavior).

My all-time favorite was *Nancy Drew*. She was my idol. I wanted to be just like her. I admired her independence, her bravery, and her blue roadster. She was the role model for a strong young woman in my generation. I received a green convertible for my sixteenth birthday, after hinting about wanting a blue roadster years ahead of time. This year, I received a pair of Nancy Drew pajamas for Mother's Day, also at my request. Nancy has been a life-long influence on me.

Each week in the summertime when I was growing up, I trekked across town to the public library and checked out eight or nine new books to read. I'll always remember what the stodgy, older woman librarian, Miss Jessie Jordan, said to me every week, "Books are your friends. Treat them with care. Wash your hands before touching a book and never turn down any pages." She was one of those guideposts in my young life, helping me get to Level III. She is the one who realized I was ready to leave the youth books and wisely introduced me to adult books at an early age. It was as if a whole new world opened up. She actually gave me permission to read in the adult section!

One author stands out vividly in my mind: Grace Livingston Hill. I would rush to her section each week to see if anyone had returned one of her books. She was a romance writer and was one of the best selling authors in the world. Not only I, but millions of readers around the world were drawn to her historical novels portraying eternal truths set in the 1900's. She was like a mother or a grandmother to me. As Jessie Jordan had reminded me as a child, books were my friends. Grace Livingston Hill was indeed a friend. I remember her as being kind. I felt warm inside while reading her work. I must have needed warmth and comfort at that time in my life, and she provided it through her words. Somehow her books comforted me.

MOTHER AS EMOTIONAL COACH

This and other things are what can happen with your child. Books and authors can have a significant impact on your child's maturation process. I hope you give your children an opportunity to have remarkable experiences with books.

When I was in high school, it was an honor in our town for one student to be selected to work at the library part-time. Miss Gertrude Mahan, our town librarian after Jessie Jordan died, interviewed and selected me. I was in nirvana for an entire year, as I was surrounded by thousands of books each day I worked. I loved opening boxes of new books from the publisher. I still remember their new-book smell.

After I married and had children, I read to my children each night until they were eight or nine years old. They each belonged to a book club and we made weekly trips to the library so we would never run out of reading material. Their father told them a bedtime story every night. Our nighttime rituals were lengthy, and many a night found me sound asleep in the third child's bed.

After they could read well by themselves, each child had their favorite reading genre. They were allowed to read thirty minutes after getting into bed, then after their night-time kisses from us, they shut off their bedside lamp and went to sleep.

Blake loved fantasy. He read everything by C.S. Lewis and was a *Dungeons and Dragons* fan. Later, he was entranced by Robert Ludlum. As an adult, he has read every Harry Potter book. Ashley devoured all the *Little House on the Prairie* books, as well as anything about horses. Trent loved reading about World War II and became an expert on it by fourth grade. He read the Time-Life series on the subject, plus practically memorized the encyclopedia articles about generals in the war.

I hope you make a production about reading at your house. I hope your children see you reading in your leisure time. I hope you turn off the television, Game Boy, Play Station, computer, and other electronic entertainment devices on a regular basis so your family can spend quiet time reading, then perhaps discussing what each person has read. It seems rather old-fashioned, but I hope you try it so you can see the benefits derived from it.

Your children need this time. They need to be quiet. They need to learn to entertain themselves. It helps them develop emotionally.

Summary:
    You can guide your child to emotional development.
    Your child needs quiet time to read.
    Talking about books with your child is important.
    Turning off electronic devices is a good thing.
    Your child can learn about herself by reading good literature.

Something to think about:

1. Think of your reading experiences as a child and what books made a positive impact on your development. Share these experiences and books with your child.

2. Talk to your child about what he is reading. Ask questions and listen carefully to the answers. This will tell you volumes about how he is developing and how he is beginning to have significant thoughts about life's meaning for himself.

3. Plan weekly trips to the library, bookstore, or other literary gatherings for children. Take your child to hear authors speak. You never know what life-long impact this might have on his emotional development.

CHAPTER 5

Principle Five: You must help your children quiet their minds, unclutter their lives, and cut down on their activities

I am continuing the story about volunteering in Jonestown at the beginning of this chapter. I hope you noticed it was missing from the last chapter. The reason it was missing is that Chapter Four is about reading. There was little to no reading happening in Jonestown. There were no books in the McKnight household. That made me sad.

Remember, also, how I was going to tell you about the guilt I felt in Jonestown. That made me sad, too.

No Swimming Pool

The first day we went swimming in Clarksdale, I thought nothing of it. I walked to the McKnight house, picked up my swim bag, walked back to the convent, and off we drove for a well-deserved swim and relaxation.

The pool at the Comfort Inn was nothing to write home about. It was a 12' x 20' concrete rectangle with old-fashioned green and white striped lounge chairs scattered around it, a few of the straps missing or hanging loose. There was no landscaping, just the pool. I didn't care.

I felt liberated. I had been sweltering all day long and the water felt *refreshing. I would gladly have paid for the privilege of playing in the cool water. Later, sitting beside the pool in a lounge chair, I enjoyed exchanging experiences of the day with my fellow volunteers. Each of us had poignant stories to tell of a particular child we worked with that day.*

"What would you think if I chose eight children tomorrow to do an art project with me?" I asked.

"Tell us about the project," they inquired.

"I saw several kids today who look like they have some real artistic talent and I thought it would be fun to make a painted mural of Jonestown, showing their houses, the downtown, school, and their church."

"Great idea," they echoed.

"I promise to keep some of the live wires occupied," I declared, as we all laughed, knowing exactly who we were talking about.

Before we drove back to Jonestown that evening, we stopped at Wal-Mart to buy a roll of poster paper and poster paints.

I was excited about the project and couldn't wait to get there the next day so the children and I could get to work on it. To tell you the truth, I didn't want to spend the whole week doing puzzles, playing board games, and constructing purple dinosaurs. I'm very product-oriented, so the mural project fit my style perfectly. It would be a four-day project and we could complete it by Friday.

The next morning, I chose eight children of various ages, explained the project, and asked if they would make a commitment to work each day with me on the art team. This meant they would give up all the other optional activities. All eight agreed to the bargain and were eager to get started.

I chose an older boy, Cameron, to make the basic layout on graph paper while the younger children drew pencil sketches of their own house. Other children wandered over to the project and made pictures of their houses. Finally, we decided who would draw the church, community center, businesses on main street, schools, and other public buildings. By the end of the day, we had a basic plan sketched out on our twelve-foot mural.

MOTHER AS EMOTIONAL COACH

After cleaning up the community center, it was time to head for ye ol' swimmin' hole. This day it was different. Jeremy and DeVante were home when I went into the house for my swim bag. It was obvious where I was going. Suddenly it struck me—these kids don't have anywhere to go swimming. There isn't a swimming pool in this town. Kids don't even have wading pools in their yard. A sudden flood of guilt rushed over me. Here I was, hot, sticky, and tired. I could go swimming to relieve the misery of a hot summer's day. Jeremy and DeVante were hot, sticky, and tired, too. All they could do was stand on the porch and wave as I walked away. I'll always remember the sad and disappointed look in their eyes. Even though it was against the rules, I wanted to get a car and take them swimming somewhere. Instead, I simply cried. Oh, and don't forget the guilt part.

Children in Jonestown don't expect to go swimming.

Slow down your life

Your children probably have not been without a swimming pool in your town or city. In fact, you might even have one in your own back yard. At our house, we didn't have one in our back yard, but our dog had his own plastic wading pool. Our children were at the neighborhood pool every day of their lives in the summer months. All their friends were there. All my friends were there. The pool was our social center and we loved it.

There are certain adjustments you need to make so that your child can experience happiness. You might be wondering what makes your child happy way down deep. What makes him happy is doing nothing. I know this is hard for you to stomach. Busyness is like an addiction. If you're not busy, something must be wrong with you. Your child has no friends. You feel isolated and wonder what to do. I wonder what you would do if there were nothing to do. I wonder what your child would do if there were no scheduled activities vying for his time and energy.

"Monkey mind" is a Buddhist term, referring to mental activity that

YOU MUST HELP YOUR CHILDREN QUIET THEIR MINDS

creates busyness which keeps us away from our true self. Look at our whole busy culture and see how it is built on busyness. This is not the road to happiness, neither for your child nor for yourself.

I remember many lazy summer mornings when the kids slept as late as they wanted, then got up and had a leisurely breakfast. Later on in the morning, they went straight from their pajamas to their swimsuits, eagerly awaiting the opening of the pool. We called it "hanging out." We weren't really doing anything—reading the paper, making a few phone calls, doing some household tasks. But as I look back on it, it was fun. We had an opportunity to talk, and perhaps to watch a game show on TV together.

What makes a child happy

Happiness, to a child, is not driving around all day long, rushing from one activity to the next, while you are on the cell phone calling ahead to explain why you are running late.

Happiness, to a child, is simple. Of course, he thinks he has to have every gadget and toy he sees on his favorite cartoon show to make him happy. Having his senses bombarded 18 hours a day by media or loud music prevents happiness. He may think these things will make him happy, but they don't. They don't, because all they are doing is creating in him a desire for the next gadget or whatever Johnny down the street owns. And, they are numbing his mind.

If you'll be honest with yourself, you know that materialism is rampant in your neighborhood, and you're trying to hold your nose above water to keep up with it. Even if you have strong feelings against materialism and rushing around from one activity to another, it's difficult for you to say "no" when "all my friends are doing it or having it."

You hear yourself saying how busy you are. All your friends are saying it, too. It's like a badge of honor. The busier you are and the more activities your children are in, supposedly the better a person and parent you are. This could not be further from the truth.

◂ MOTHER AS EMOTIONAL COACH

Making choices

When our children were growing up, I worked as an educator, had a large house to keep, and in general, had my hands full. I came to the conclusion, in order to maintain my sanity, each child could participate in only two activities. Frankly, that's all the time I had. There was only so much time in the week, and I was willing to drive only so many miles transporting kids to their activities.

Luckily, all three chose soccer and piano lessons. Even luckier, two of them could be on the same soccer team and all three could go to their piano lessons on the same day. This simplified my life considerably.

I'll always remember the summer, however, when we had three children on three different softball teams in three different towns. Talk about a scheduling nightmare! Oh, and besides the twice-a-week games, there were weekly practices. It was enough to make a time-management expert pull out her hair. My husband and I had a strict transportation schedule every evening and we could not waver from it. I was never so glad to see a season come to an end. We were on overload and we weren't happy.

What our children remember the most about summer were the nights we stayed home, cooked dinner together, ate out on the deck, cleaned up the dishes, then went back outside to look for satellites passing by in the night sky. My husband gave a quarter for each one spotted. At the same time, we were listening to the baseball game on the radio, chatting and laughing the night away. We took turns holding the dog, who was in dog heaven when the family was together, and so were we. We were happy. Doing nothing.

Families and nature

Lately, I have seen families biking together, walking along the streamway trail together, eating picnics together, and fishing together. I especially liked the fishing family because the children were pre-schoolers, yet so excited, each holding a small pole their father had baited. They were happy.

Simple things make you happy.

YOU MUST HELP YOUR CHILDREN QUIET THEIR MINDS

Your child's personal philosophy is formulated while she is young. If she is reaching for Level III of Dabrowski's Theory of Positive Disintegration, she needs plenty of time to contemplate the dichotomy between how she wants the world to be versus the way it seems to be. Having quiet time is one of the best ways you can help her with this urgent concern. Having quiet time in nature is even better.

Some children will find solace in having a deep connection to the out-of-doors while spending time there; others will like the ocean or sailing; still others might discover the principles of life while looking through a telescope at the starry night. These and many other inspiring adventures help them discover their life path. This path will probably not be discovered while sitting in the back of your SUV driving to yet another activity.

Summary:
    Limit your child's activities.
    Minimize materialism in your family.
    Maximize family time spent at home.
    Provide quiet time for your children.
    Spend time in nature with your family.

Some things to think about:

1. Think about your family's activities. Imagine what your life might be like if you eliminated some of them. Limit your children's choices in activities.

2. Look around your house and notice how much how much clutter there is and how many unnecessary items you own. Think about how you and your children could make someone less fortunate happy by sharing some of your possessions.

3. Create fun adventures in nature for your family. Notice how happy you feel. Repeat similar adventures until it becomes natural for you to be together having fun—doing not much of anything.

CHAPTER **6**

Principle Six: Intuition is your best teacher

Now that you have the kids out of the car, have determined priorities for your time, and have rid your home your home of unnecessary objects, I'll bet you're wondering how you're going to proceed with the foreign idea of doing nothing.

It's easy. Let your intuition be your guide. Intuition is the ability to tap into thoughts essential to one's well-being. Unlike your other five senses— touch, sight, smell, hearing, and taste— intuition is not processed through your intellect. Intuition perceives things without relying on your senses. It's a way to gain information—knowing without knowing how you know. Intuition just knows. Everyone has the capacity for intuition.

You probably haven't been listening to your intuition for quite awhile. You've been busy. Busy with babies, busy with work, busy cooking, busy doing yardwork—a hundred kind of busies. You've been so busy you haven't had time to listen to yourself.

Listening to yourself is one of the best ways to spend your time. Your intuition will kick in if it thinks you're listening.

Sit it out

One of my best teachers on the topic of intuition is Gary Zukav. In 1989, he wrote a book, *The Seat of the Soul*. His basic premise is if you sit on the seat of your soul long enough, you can resolve your negative feelings and emotions. Sitting on the seat of your soul means to stop what you're doing and pay attention to your inner voice. Listen to what is being said to you. To me, this means I need to take a break. I've been running on empty. My body and mind are rebelling. I need to jump off the merry-go-round and unwind.

Since reading Zukav's book, I have incorporated a new method of dealing with problems. Instead of running away from negative feelings by engaging in as many activities as there are hours in my waking day, now I take time to feel those feelings. Last week, for example, I had a busy week. By Wednesday evening, I realized I needed to put the brakes on my flitting.

On Thursday morning, I took a long walk on a hiking trail near my house. It felt exhilarating to be out of doors enjoying nature instead of getting up early, hurriedly dressing, then racing off in the car to meet someone else's schedule. The world didn't miss me and I was feeling much more in tune with myself and more ready to continue with my life.

When I take time out, I am more aware of how I am feeling. If I am depressed, I feel it deeply. I befriend it. I listen to it. I am especially kind to myself. I practice extreme self-care by eating healthy, exercising, and getting plenty of sleep. I no longer fight with the feeling of depression, thinking there is something wrong with me when I feel the despair. I take time to relax and guess what? I do nothing. I give my body an opportunity to realign itself. Then the depression departs. I have, at long last, learned to accept depression as just another part of what makes me human.

Mothers are susceptible to depression, mostly because you begin to feel like a machine. You are up in the morning, going all day into the night, and finally, at long last, it's time to go to bed so you can get up in the morning and do it all over again. You need some solitude for yourself.

When my children were small, I lived for mother's day out. It was only one day a week, from 10:00 a.m. until 3:00 p.m. but it was precious time to call my own. You'll be a better parent when you allow yourself some space to breathe and do nothing. Your children will be fine without you for awhile. Let your husband or mother-in-law take over child care for awhile. Your children don't need you every minute. Give yourself permission to be selfish. They'll benefit from it, too.

Clear each day emotionally

When I take time to acknowledge my negative feelings, they pass right through me, and are replaced by much better feelings. You can help your children learn to do this, even at an early age. When my children were growing up, I spent hours with each one at various times when they were upset. I would go to their bedroom at night and we would talk over incidents of the day that I knew were still bothering them. This is called clearing each day of emotional impacts. Don't let your son go to bed angry or hurt. Help him let go of what's bothering him.

At our house, we were a family with high emotions. We let it all hang out. I had to make many apologies to our children for things I said or did. My husband was prone to quick bursts of temper, followed by calmness and a quick return to normal. Our children were objects of some of his outbursts. After such an explosion, they usually sulked up to their rooms, hurt and angry.

I took it upon myself to convince my husband he had probably hurt them, then insisted he go upstairs and apologize before the children went to sleep. I remember watching him trudge up the stairs, dreading to face their hurt feelings. My point was: nothing a child said or did deserved a hurtful response from her parent.

Obviously, this was not one of the happy evenings I have described

INTUITION IS YOUR BEST TEACHER

in a previous chapter. We are talking about a tense evening, especially as the teen years loomed. All of those trudgings and apologies paid off in the long run, though, when we look at the individuals they are today.

If emotional outbursts are happening in your home, remember—*you* are the emotional coach. It is your job as mother to make sure your children are emotionally balanced. It's up to you to help make emotional hurts dissipate for your children. You are the only one in their lives who can do this. You're wired for it. It's up to you to stabilize your home.

Yes, it's difficult. Yes, it takes time. I hope you take the responsibility of setting things right emotionally with your children, or insist their father do the same if he's the one in the wrong.

Many times, you will be called upon to help your child to deal with emotional zingers that happen outside the home. One year, when my daughter was in the fifth grade, she and I spent several evenings talking about her teacher. After much discussion, she said, "My teacher doesn't like me."

Although I seldom called my children's teachers, I decided this was one of those times. When I shared Ashley's sad remark, I could hear compassion and empathy in her teacher's reply. She told me she would get it straightened out the next day.

Emotional channels

If you help keep your child's emotional channels open, this leads him to have an open heart and brings him closer to unconditional love, thus allowing intuition to flow through him. Intuition is a sixth sense and a knowledge that will see him through rough times, because, you see, intuitive knowledge is not processed the way intellectual knowledge is processed. It is not processed at all. It simply *is*.

Intuition becomes an inner fortress in times of trouble and stress. When he trusts his intuition, he is asking for guidance and he will receive it. It is a sensory system which operates on its own without input from his other five senses.

MOTHER AS EMOTIONAL COACH

One thing you have to do as a parent is to trust your *own* intuition, and even moreover than that, encourage your child to trust his. One of the greatest gifts you can give your child is the ability to think through things independently and to draw conclusions based on knowledge he doesn't know he possesses.

Opening the door to intuition

If you can teach your child the basic facts of nutrition and if she is making an attempt to follow them, keep in mind you are also helping her intuition. Her mind must be clear in order to listen and to respond to intuition. It can't be clear if she's surviving on pizza, soda, and candy bars.

An essential thing you can do as a parent is to insist upon a proper nutritional program. No matter how many times your child wants a quadruple order of French fries and a greasy cheeseburger, you must resist (most of the time). You set the example by how you eat, how you cook, whether you snack or not, and in general, by your relationship with food.

Don't follow every diet fad that comes down the pike. Each food and food group was put on this earth to eat. Don't put the idea into your child's head that there are good foods and bad foods. There are acceptable and unacceptable ways to prepare foods, so I hope you are setting a good example by cooking with good nutrition in mind.

Another way to cultivate your own and your child's intuition is to be open toward life and to hold a sense that there is a reason for all that is happening, and that at the heart of the reason lies compassion and goodness. Be a bloomin' optimist, no matter what others say or think. Your children are watching, you know, and don't you want them to be open to the world and its goodness?

Listening to intuition

I'm sure you have read stories about people who had a bad feeling about getting on a certain flight, then something tragic happened on that flight.

I'll bet you want your daughter to have a sharp intuition when a gentleman approaches her in the mall, says he wants to help her become a model, and would she come out to his car to sign some papers. Teach your child to listen to her intuition, her inner radar guiding her through tricky situations.

This spring I was invited to judge a national entrepreneurial competition for college students. I loved being there, was energized by the students' presentations, and later learned the winners earned the right to compete at the international competition. Upon inquiring, I discovered I qualified to judge the international finals in Barcelona, Spain. I was excited and looked forward to going in the early fall.

However, my intuition was telling me something else. It was telling me not to get a plane ticket, and not to plan on going. I've been trusting my intuition for a long time, but this time I didn't want to. From experience, I knew not to go against my intuition, so I begrudgingly stopped looking for the best fare to Barcelona on cheaptickets.com.

In July, I received a phone call from my son in California saying he and his family were moving in September and asking if I would help. In August, I received a call from my daughter, who lives in the same city as my son, asking me to help her move during the same period of time. *Thank you, intuition, for one more time knowing more than I know and for talking me into making the right decision.* This intuition thing happens to me frequently because I listen to it and I trust it. Therefore, I guess it trusts me.

Intuition serves

Another way my intuition served me was during my doctoral studies. When I came to the point of writing my dissertation, I hardly had to go to the library or to the internet for references. All I had to do was go to my home library. Evidently, for several years, I had been collecting most of the books I would need, all without knowing it. Something knew, though—my intuition. I appreciate that thing. When you slow down and start listening to your intuition, you are going to be amazed where it will lead you.

◄ MOTHER AS EMOTIONAL COACH

Intuition and creativity

Intuition can serve you and your child. One way it serves me is with my creativity. Sometimes I get an insight or an inspiration, but I have no idea where it came from. It's usually when I've been working hard on a project and the thought fits right in with what I'm doing. Sometimes I want a creative impulse, and I need to jump-start my mind. That's when I turn to some of the funniest people I know, such as Ashleigh Brilliant, former nationally syndicated cartoonist. After reading a few of his Brilliant Thoughts like, "I have abandoned my search for truth, and am now looking for a good fantasy," or "I may not be totally perfect, but parts of me are excellent," I am laughing.

Laughter opens the door to intuition and creativity for me. Some other funny people I like in the media are Gary Larson (*The Far Side*), Dave Barry (*Miami Herald*), and Cathy Guisewite, syndicated cartoonist.

Sark is an artist I admire. She gets my creative juices flowing when I spend time with her book called, *Sark's Journal and Play! Book: A Place to Dream While Awake*. She also has other books, such as *Living Juicy* and *Inspiration Sandwich*. These delectable books make room for intuition to occur.

I hope you spend time with your children just messing around. It's so much fun and you are creating priceless memories. One of my favorite photos in the family album is a scene in our kitchen where Ashley is creating an item with yarn, Trent is painting, and Blake is baking. Our kitchen looks like an artist's workshop. I'm glad we took the time for those simple home activities.

Playing the piano also opens the door to my intuition and creativity. It relaxes me. I concentrate on the notes as I create beautiful music; well, most of the time, if I happen to be hitting the right notes that day.

I also like yoga. Your child might like yoga. Yoga for kids is the rage right now. Of course, don't expect to see it in the public schools, as some people think it is a religion and will not allow their child to participate in it. If you don't hold these beliefs, perhaps you could get some mats, a yoga DVD, and try it. My friend, Suzanne, does yoga with her granddaughter, Alex. Alex loves it, and it's a great bonding experience for the two of them.

Intuition is helping me write this book. This is my first book, so I didn't know how to go about it. I decided to sit down and start writing, even if it was wrong. I knew I wanted to share the conclusions of my dissertation, but I wasn't sure how to conceptualize it so it didn't sound like academic writing. Suddenly, I found myself writing about some experiences I hadn't thought about for years. It also occurred to me to incorporate the story of Jonestown so you could see a sharp contrast to your life and how we all need to give service to others.

If you listen to your intuition, you may have a happier, healthier life. And, as I told you before, if momma's happy and emotionally developed, chances are your children will be happy and emotionally developed. You will have an opportunity to hear your children say, "I came from a stable home," after they leave your home to establish their own stable home for your grandchildren.

Children who live in Jonestown, Mississippi, probably rely on their intuition in various situations. They are left alone much of the time and learn to fend for themselves. A strong sense of intuition can keep them out of trouble as they lead their self-sufficient lives. I think they used intuition while doing the mural project as well.

Stable Homes Help Us Cope

Just the other evening, I was sitting out on the patio on a starry, summer evening with two neighbor women. We were eating cheese, crackers, fruits, nuts, and drinking wine together, while having a candid conversation about ourselves and our lives.

Pat told about how, thirty-four years ago, she became pregnant after her sophomore year in college. Her parents gave her three choices: get an abortion, drive across the state line and get married so the notice wouldn't

MOTHER AS EMOTIONAL COACH

appear in the local paper of her small town, or go stay with her grandmother in California, have the baby, and give it up for adoption. She agonized about the decision, but finally decided on marrying the baby's father.

On this particular night, she wondered aloud how her daughter, Becky, would have turned out if she had let her go for adoption. Becky and her two children bring joy to Pat's life. Thinking about life without her is impossible.

Gretchen, the other neighbor, recounted her life with a mentally-ill husband, who, after thirty-odd years of marriage, is now in a nursing home. They remain married because a divorce would be too complicated.

I shared the story of my son, Trent, who was killed in an auto accident when he was a senior in high school, and how his death continues to affect my daughter, Ashley, his twin sister. His death never goes away for us. It has had far-reaching effects on our entire family, including my former husband, who was my husband when Trent died.

"How have we all survived and how are we all still well-adjusted?" asked Gretchen. Answering her own question, she said, "In my case, I know it's because of my father and how good he was to me."

"I came from a stable home," answered Pat. "I learned from an early age to take responsibility for what happens to me, and to move on."

"My father was supportive of me in every way," I volunteered. "He always treated me like someone special. He talked to me about how he solved his problems. I learned to overcome adversity because I saw how he handled it."

"Isn't it amazing that all three of us have had tragedy in our lives, yet we're still all basically okay?" asked Gretchen.

"It takes that strong family background to withstand life's storms," I surmised.

"Everyone has heartaches and troubles." Pat added. "Growing up in a stable family helps you make it through the tough times."

We all nodded in agreement.

INTUITION IS YOUR BEST TEACHER

I hope you use your intuition to maintain a stable home for your family.

Summary:
 It's okay to do nothing.
 Listen to your intuition.
 Allow your intuition to guide you.
 Trust your intuition.
 Trust your child's intuition.
 It's up to you to stabilize your home.

Something to think about:

1. Recall a time when you listened to and followed your intuition. If you can't make this recollection, begin to listen to your inner voice and follow it, even a little bit. Every time you trust it, you will gain more confidence in using it to make important decisions in your life.

2. Plan some simple creative activities with your children. Don't worry about the mess it makes. Creativity isn't neat. You can scrub the floor later—and perhaps replace household items marred by creating. You're making something much more valuable than your antique kitchen table.

3. Make it a point each day to clear the emotional air before everyone goes to bed. You'll feel better for it and so will everyone else. It's your job as emotional coach.

CHAPTER 7

Principle Seven: Your child will thrive and develop a wider range of emotions if he feels your support and unconditional love.

One of our goals in Global Volunteers is to be totally committed to supporting local people in their struggle to become self-reliant. In doing our volunteer work, we must fully respect the host community's inherent wisdom and potential. We are merely guests in the community who will do the work requested. I discovered that being a servant leader in Mississippi, on the island of Oahu, and in Costa Rica helped me develop unconditional love for people in cultures that are different from mine.

Finishing the mural

By Friday, our creative work group of eight rambunctious girls and boys, ages six to twelve, had worked, argued, discussed, laughed, and painted their way to a twelve-foot-long masterpiece. They carefully taped it to the wall as the last day of camp ended. Their faces beamed with pride. They shyly received compliments from their fellow campers. The mural was a beautiful tribute to their teamwork. What we saw before us was how the children envisioned their town. They had used their intuition in creating it, instead of using photographs as models.

YOUR CHILD WILL THRIVE AND DEVELOP A WIDER RANGE OF EMOTIONS

The mural was born of their imaginations and it was a colorful replica of how they envisioned Jonestown. Instead of drab, unpainted houses, the mural houses were multi-hued. Civic buildings looked inviting, with their open doors and flags flying out in front. Laughing people filled the neighborhoods and the streets were lined with cars. Green lawns and flowers framed the front of each house. Children who hadn't worked on the mural took turns guessing which house was theirs.

Saturday afternoon was the art show. What began as an empty, stark room on Monday was now transformed into a gallery of colorful drawings which demonstrated the children's artistic endeavors. At 3 p.m., parents and children arrived.

Mothers wearing colorful dresses came up the stairs holding hands with their child. I barely recognized the children, dressed in their finest clothes. Boys wearing starched shirts and creased slacks broke away from their mothers and slid across the room on their slick-bottomed dress shoes. Girls, hair braided and interlaced with ribbons, wore frilly dresses with fancy white patent shoes and lacy stockings. Rhythmically, they rocked back and forth on their heels and toes, making tapping noises on the linoleum floor, as they admired the boys' athletic prowess.

The Global Volunteers decorated the room with streamers and balloons. We served fruit punch and had purchased a large colorfully-frosted cake. Each child was on her best behavior as she pointed out her own contribution to the art show. We had taught them how to make introductions so we could meet their parents. We practiced the day before.

With little prompting, each camper introduced his parent to us. Every parent thanked us profusely for what we had done for their son or daughter. They were grateful for the opportunity we gave their child.

After the party, as I swept the floor and emptied trash, I recalled the thought I realized when I first arrived: the children in Jonestown needed more than we could ever give them. There was great potential in that

MOTHER AS EMOTIONAL COACH

roomful of children, but the poverty and lack of economic opportunity we observed seemed overwhelming.

Earlier in the week, I had walked over to the elementary school to ask the principal if I could laminate the mural and mail it to him. He said he'd be happy to have it and he would hang it in the cafeteria when it arrived.

It was my hope that when school started in the fall, as the children looked at the mural each day, they would remember the joy, fun, and unconditional love we had shared that hot week in August.

You and unconditional love

Those words are easy to say, more difficult to do. Unconditional love means loving a child under even the most difficult of circumstances. It is the space we create for her to be who she is. Sometimes the little person she is has her own strong will and is determined to have her own way. That's when it's tough to love her.

It's easy to love a baby, who coos and smiles as you bathe her, smelling delicious and feeling cuddly after you diaper and dress her. It gets trickier when she gets older and embarrasses you in public with a temper tantrum. At times like this, you feel like giving her to the next person who walks by and then running to the car, dying from embarrassment.

Unconditional love means you will always love your child, even though you dislike her behavior at times. It means you will tell her, after that embarrassing scene, "I didn't like your behavior at the shopping center. Because of your inappropriate behavior, we won't be going to the ice cream store like we had planned." Then you apply those consequences, even though it might be inconvenient for you, because you really, really wanted a chocolate raspberry truffle ice cream cone.

YOUR CHILD WILL THRIVE AND DEVELOP A WIDER RANGE OF EMOTIONS

There's nothing worse than thinking you're a bad parent. Well, maybe it's having strangers think you're a bad parent after your child's public display of inappropriate behavior. My children's behavior has humiliated me more times than I can count. In fact, one time I lost it badly when I made the mistake of taking all three of them into a department store. They started playing hide and seek under the clothing racks and were having so much fun they wouldn't stop running, laughing, and acting like rascals.

I felt humiliated and yanked them out of the store. Realizing it was my own fault that I had put them in that situation, I felt irrational and overwhelmed.

Unconditional love for yourself

I needed to give myself some unconditional love at that moment, but all I could do was blame myself. I considered running away from home. Here I was, an educated professional and I couldn't manage my own children's behavior. I felt inadequate and unprepared as a mother. I wanted to get into the car, drive away, and never look back. Somehow I came to my senses, probably after they were all tucked safely into their beds and were acting sweet again. I imagine you have felt this same way. Or even worse. This is where unconditional love and patience comes in handy—also a few deep breaths and a quick exit out of the situation.

Last week at yoga, there was a new young woman in our class. After class, I said, "I'm glad you came today and hope you come back next week."

"Oh, I'll be back, all right. I stay home with a two-year-old, and I need this class to help keep my wits about me."

"I know what you mean. I've been there myself. It's tough. *But it's worth it.*"

MOTHER AS EMOTIONAL COACH

Staying home with your child

Staying home with children was not my idea. I was on the fast track in my educational career. I was going to teach for a few years while I worked toward an administrative degree, then become a principal. Later, I could become a district administrator, an educational consultant, and author.

After my son was born, I stayed out of the work-force for more than a year. I thought that bonding time would give him a good start in life, then I could go back to my job as an elementary school teacher. I did go back to work after that year and taught for 1 ½ more years, at which time I was six months pregnant with twins and was confined to bed rest for the last three months.

There was no way I could consider going back to work with three children under three years of age. There were no nannies available to come into our home. That would have been perfect, but that was not possible. Instead, I would have had to get three small children changed, dressed, fed, put into car seats, taken out of car seats, and into the day care facility, all before eight a.m. I just couldn't imagine myself doing that. It made me tired thinking about it. After giving myself a huge pep talk and readjusting my work attitude, I actually enjoyed being a full-time mom. I'm not saying it was easy. It wasn't.

Lots of times, I felt like the Pied Piper, with my entourage following me everywhere I went. I wished just once I could take a shower without someone banging on the door and needing me for something. It's hard to act loving when you can't even go to the bathroom alone.

Managing children takes energy, energy that sometimes you'd like to expend playing tennis or going shopping. Keep in mind, you will have many years after your children are out of the house to do whatever your heart desires. Right now, it's your job to give unconditional love in the form of time, energy, and resources. You must give your child the best you have to offer.

Unconditional love places the emotional needs of the child first. You

YOUR CHILD WILL THRIVE AND DEVELOP A WIDER RANGE OF EMOTIONS

cannot discipline a child effectively unless your primary relationship with him is one based on unconditional love. He needs the strong foundation of your acceptance of him as an individual, just the way he is. Development of his behavior and emotional stability is your responsibility.

In contrast to your total life span, the time you spend raising your family is not that long. I think it's worth it to give it your all during that period of your life.

Think of your future life span and imagine how you can eventually have it all. Plot out five-year segments and what you will be doing at that particular time. These young years with children are tough on you. It won't always be that way.

This is not to say you won't have meaningful work while your children are small.

For example, I used the time while I was at home with my pre-schoolers to work on my master's degree. My classes were in the late afternoon, so I hired a high-school girl to stay with the children for an hour until their father came home from work.

Later on, I took a course in tax preparation and worked part-time when my husband could watch the kids during the cold, winter months. As you know, days inside with small children can get long.

Signs of the times

Latest data tells us that 21% of moms who are college graduates are home with their kids (*Pew Reports*, 2012.) This means a large percentage of you moms are more willing to sacrifice paychecks and prestige for time with your families than were young moms in the past.

You realize you can't have it all—all at the same time, that is. You might choose to drop out of the career track for a few years, but you fully intend to step back in at a later time in your child's life. Others of you will discover new talents while you're a stay-at-home mom. You can turn these talents into a new business, never returning to working for someone else again.

When you're tired

Let's say you aren't one of the moms who chose to stay home with your small children. Let's say you have a nanny who is loving and capable. What then? I'll bet you're still worried and perhaps feel a bit guilty about possibly shortchanging your child. And, I'll bet you're tired.

I remember many days, after I went back to teaching, when I would wake up still tired and yearning for night-time to return so I could get back to sleep. I was exhausted. That wasn't a good way to live my life. I should have relaxed more and taken some of the advice I've been giving you in this book, but I just kept on trucking down the road—tired. We probably could have done without my full-time income. I could have taught part-time. There was no sense in me being constantly tired.

It's difficult to give unconditional love when you're tired, but you can. You must.

Summary:
It's your job to give unconditional love.
Just because your kids act out, it doesn't mean you're a bad parent.
Give your child the best you have to offer when he needs it most.
You can have it all, but not at the same time.
Don't live your life exhausted.

Something to think about:

1. You must learn to give yourself unconditional love because you can't give to your child what you don't have for yourself. Write down all the wonderful qualities you have. Look at your qualities

YOUR CHILD WILL THRIVE AND DEVELOP A WIDER RANGE OF EMOTIONS

so you can actually see yourself as you really are. Ask your friends or relatives to tell you what they see when they see you.

2. Practice speaking aloud all of the things you deserve, such as respect and attention to your needs. Action preceeds behavior, and when your subconscious hears what you deserve, it starts believing them. You must do this work. Noone else can do it for you. You're in charge of your own unconditional love.

3. Plan time to rest. Your house doesn't have to be perfect. Your laundry doesn't have to be folded and put away right now if you are exhausted. Work will wait. Your attitude and frame of mind are in direct proportion to the amount of sleep you get. You can't give unconditional love to anyone in an exhausted state.

CHAPTER 8

Principle Eight: You and your child can become empowered through praying.

I'm going to be honest with you. When I realized the last principle was about praying, I felt intrepidation. I have a sad and sorry prayer life, according to what I read and according to people who go to prayer groups. My prayer life is along the lines of Anne LaMott, who has three prayers: Thank You, Help Me, and Wow!

In my prayer theology, God is omnipotent and knows all, so I don't need to reiterate to God what He already knows. I do pray for people who are ill, are grieving, need help, or have had some tragedy befall them, so intercessory prayer is something I do.

I don't believe God is a popularity contest, as in whomever gets the most prayers, He saves, heals, or lets live. Can't you just see the big computer in the sky tallying up the numbers, then printing off the names of the people who won the prayer contest? That is not my idea of God.

I was an utter failure when it came to teaching my children to pray. Oh, we went to church and they went to church school, then vacation church school in the summer. They attended every summer Bible camp within a five-mile radius of our house. It was that baby-sitting thing—anything to have a few hours to myself. I'll bet you can relate to that.

YOU AND YOUR CHILD CAN BECOME EMPOWERED THROUGH PRAYING

I felt like a hypocrite, praying with them after I had been yelling at them all day, correcting them for this and that misbehavior, like a sergeant with her troops. Then to turn around and pray—well, that didn't seem quite right to me. Perhaps it was just an excuse. I don't know what it was, but I do know I didn't do it.

Maturing in our prayer life

One little prayer we used to say at mealtime went like this: God is great. God is good. Let us thank Him for this food. Well, that's just fine for pre-schoolers and younger elementary kids. It seems, however, that older kids and teens could become more sophisticated in their prayers. Not at our house.

Dreading to write this chapter, I put it off, until, if I were going to finish this book, I had to face my failure. Yes, I admit it. I was a failure at helping develop my children's prayer life. No wonder my children never went beyond the "God is great" prayer. I was stammering, stuttering, and didn't know what to say in my own prayers, and I was their model.

I pray like a banshee now. I pray at the drop of a hat. I was a chaplain at the University of Kansas Medical Center for thirteen years. I guess I had to overcome my own bugaboos about prayer in order to start praying for real. My prayers for the patients in the hospital always had the same theme: Thy will be done. I never asked God for anything except for the patient to feel peace and love. I didn't pray for them unless they asked me to. I just didn't want to get in the long line of requests at God's popularity contest.

Early religious education

When I was growing up, our family was religious—very religious. We went to Sunday school and church on Sunday morning, then usually had some church activity during the week. I was in the church choir beginning in elementary school and continued with it until I graduated from high school. I attended Vacation Bible School each summer. I learned Bible

MOTHER AS EMOTIONAL COACH

verses because we received a Hershey's bar if we learned and recited a certain amount of them.

Middle-school youngsters are a handful. I guarantee I was. I can honestly say that from about age 10 on, I was what they call "oppositionally defiant." I was just fine as long at no one tried to cross me or tried to make me do something I didn't want to do, but when either of these things happened—BANG! There was trouble and plenty of it.

It was during those years that my mother died and my father re-married. Lois did not like me, not one little bit. I explained earlier how she solved the problem named ME. We fought and I scratched and kicked. One night, after a particularly defiant event, Lois and Daddy came into my room and told me they were going to pray for me.

My purpose in telling you this is: DON'T DO IT. If they had come into my room and said, "Stephany, we are having all kinds of problems getting along. We love you and want you to pray with us to ask God for peace and harmony in our home. Would you like to do that with us?" I might have considered this soft-handed approach to God.

The way they did it, however, was in a manner that told me there was something wrong with me and God needed to fix me. Not only did this turn me off to them, it turned me off to God, which was exactly the opposite of what they were trying to do.

Never, never, and I repeat, NEVER try to use God to manipulate your children. They will resent you and even worse, it will make them resent God. Always present God as a loving and kind Being who wants the best for your child. Leave your own hidden agendas out of it.

In high school, I was in MYF (Methodist Youth Fellowship). I went to week end MYF retreats and traveled to Colorado with our youth minister for a dude ranch experience. The main thing I remember about that week was that we were supposed to have silent meditation at night until we went to sleep. My silent meditation was interrupted each night by my camp counselor, the youth minister's wife.

The two of them would stand on the porch of our cabin and smooch for what seemed like hours and I was more interested in watching what they were doing than engaging in my silent reverie. That's a high-schooler for you. I guess you can say my religious experience was interrupted by hormones.

Prayer was frequent in our home. My father could go on for what seemed like an eternity while praying. Both of my parents were Sunday school teachers, so we spent Saturday night studying our next day's Sunday school lesson. I think it's safe to assume we were prepared when Sunday morning rolled around.

Also, in our home and in my grandparent's home, we had a wooden box sitting on the dining room table containing cards called "Promises." Every morning, each family member randomly selected one colored card. On the card was a Bible verse, which was our promise for the day. I took it seriously. I thought it was a special message for me. That daily religious habit was important to me. Each of us read our promise, then we had a prayer asking God to be with us that day and help us to do unto others as we would be done unto.

Religious education later on

To top off my early religious experiences, I then attended a religious college. My father attended a Quaker university and he wanted that experience for me. I did not want that experience, thank you. As a compromise, I chose a Methodist college, and I can tell you, I did not fit in. Many of those attending our college were there because they wanted to be a minister or a missionary. That was the farthest ambition from my mind.

I was there to have fun and to have plenty of it, especially with young men. Luckily, I became friends with others who held my same goal. We were pretty wild for that conservative college, but we didn't hold a candle to what was going on at other universities. The strict rules of our college kept us pretty much in line most of the time.

We were required to attend chapel every Tuesday morning and they took roll. You got in big trouble if you skipped it, so I was always in attendance. Sometimes I went to church on Sunday morning, sort of an extension of our Saturday night fun, looking around, seeing who was there—kind of like watching our camp counselors smooch on the porch.

What counts with God

I was exposed to many religious experiences over my childhood years, but what I didn't realize until way into adulthood, was that it is my personal relationship with God that matters. Even if I never stepped foot into a church for the rest of my life, God still loves me and is my friend.

When children question religion

Not wanting to cram religion down my children's throats, I decided to be low-key about their religious education. This turned out to be a good decision, as I learned early on that my children had their own ideas about the Bible, God, and religion.

One Sunday, as I picked up our older son, Blake, from Sunday school, I casually asked what he had done and what he had learned. "You'll never guess what they tried to make me believe, Mommy. There was this guy, Jonah, and he was swallowed by a whale, but he didn't die. He lived in the belly of the whale for a long time." And this was just age four. I knew I was in trouble right then and there as far as religion was concerned. I had bred some free thinkers who weren't going to believe just any ol' story told to them.

You probably had a different up bringing from me. How you feel about praying with your children is determined by your early experiences as a child. I remember learning the "Now I lay me down to sleep" prayer. My throat usually closed when I got to the part about "If I should die before I wake...." I didn't like that one at all. I vowed not to teach that prayer to my children.

What happens to kids

Perhaps you are wondering what happened to my children regarding religion when they became adults. Both are open-minded about it. One married a member of the Jewish faith, and the other married a Catholic. They are respectful about religion. Neither of them attends church.

My grandchildren are being raised in the Catholic faith, and I am glad. My daughter-in-law is a devout Catholic. I can see that perhaps she is teaching her children by her own attitude towards God than by her words. In the same way, I hope my children learned about God from me. If this premise is true, I would feel relieved of my religious shortcomings and failures as a parent.

Faith in Jonestown

Sunday is a big day in Jonestown. Many residents attend the various churches of the denominations represented in their town. All of us volunteers felt the strong spiritual nature of the community as we attended their services. Their music was lively and the congregation responded by clapping and shouting, "Praise the Lord" and "The Lord will provide."

They seemed to find great joy and solace in their religion. The McKnight family and their 12 week-end houseguests left for church at 11 a.m. and did not return until after 4 p.m. The length of the service and their ability to sit for such a long time is testimony to the commitment they have to their congregation.

As the week went by during my visit, I could feel the strong spirits of the people I met. Their faith permeated me. They were giving me something they didn't even know they were giving. I admired their openness in expressing their feelings, their genuine care and concern for me, their inclusive natures, and their generosity in providing us shelter and food.

By merely being themselves, they changed my life.

MOTHER AS EMOTIONAL COACH

Summary:

Your child will pick up on your sincerity, or lack of it, about praying.

If prayer is real to you, teach your child to pray and to be thankful to God.

Be open to your child's doubts about religion.

Respect your child's inner spiritual life.

How you live your life is your message to your child.

Something to think about:

1. Check out books about praying for you and your child to read together. Observe how he receives them, with eagerness or more guardedly. Choose other books according to his receptivity. Respect his questions and answer them the best you can, even if you have to say, "I really don't know the answer to that question."

2. Begin saying a brief mealtime prayer with your family, reminding all that God is the provider. Use a simple prayer, so children as young as 3 or 4 can take their turn saying it.

3. Teach your child to have gratitude. Take turns going around the table expressing specific things to be thankful about. Gradually, begin praying for others, such as sick friends or their pet's health.

Good luck with your prayer campaign. Don't give up if it isn't as successful as you imagined it would be. Also, keep your sense of humor when everyone starts giggling, like my kids did.

CHAPTER 9

What's That Big Word and What Does It Have To Do With Me?

The next five chapters will tell you what you need to know about psychomotor, sensual, intellectual, emotional, and imaginational overexcitabilities. You will discover that what you thought was aberrant in yourself or in your child is simply OE, original equipment. Your child was born with it and so were you.

The more overexciteabilities your child has and the more intense they are, the greater the potential for development. You'll be the parent of a child who is an emotional leader and is unafraid of personal growth. More on this in subsequent chapters.

To give you a feel for OE's, here are three examples of children who exhibited these behaviors:

1. During the recent election, a small child was seen crying on the nightly news. She appeared to be around four years old. When her mother had picked her up from day care, the girl started crying. When her mother asked why she was crying, the child explained that she was upset about "Bronco Bama" and "Mitts Wrongly" and wished the election was over. While she echoed the sentiments of millions, her emotional overexcitability was quite precocious.

◄ MOTHER AS EMOTIONAL COACH

2. Having given up on buying her son new clothes and then arriving home to hear how much he disliked them, a mother decided to take the boy shopping so he could pick out what he did like. As they shopped, she could see that he had a distinct sense of style. In fact, she admired his style and happily purchased several shirts and jeans for him. Relieved and tired, they arrived home and she sat down to catch up on her e-mail. A few minutes later, she realized she needed to put some clothes in the dryer. Upon entering the laundry room, she discovered her son methodically cutting every label out of every new garment. Aghast, she asked why he was doing that to his new clothes. "Because I don't want them touching me and scratching me," was his reply. This was his sensual overexcitability in action. He knew before he even put on the clothes they would bother him all day long.

3. A grandmother was driving with her four-year-old grandson in the back seat. "Grandma, how old are you when you die?" he asked. "Oh, Honey, you can be any age," she answered, giving him several examples of ages and circumstances. A few minutes later, the grandmother inquired, "Why did you ask me that question?" He replied, "Because I have alot of things of things to teach my children, and I want to be sure that I live long enough to do it." The reply rendered the grandmother speechless. That's imaginational OE! Furthermore, in the words of Howard Gardner (*Theory of Multiple Intelligences*), that's also existential intelligence. Not many four-year-olds are thinking along those lines.

OE's are innate genetic predispositions of the nervous system which respond more frequently and more intensely to life's stimuli. Children with strong OE's have more intense than usual experiences in life. Dabrowski called overexcitability a tragic gift, as both and lows and highs of life are intensified. The positive side is that OE's can lead to creativity, as well as advanced emotional and ethical development.

Overexcitabilities are the stepping stones of the levels in Dabrowski's Theory. The more your child has and the more intense they are, the greater the potential for development. If this sounds like more than you signed on for, it probably is. On the other hand, it makes your job as a parent more fun, extremely exciting, and infinitely more challenging, as you strive to guide your spirited and supersensitive child along the path toward greater accomplishment and to leading a more interesting life.

Children with OE's have an abundance of physical, sensual, imaginational, intellectual, and emotional energy. They have a rich, complex, and turbulent inner experience. They live with great joy and great frustration.

The joys of being overexcitable need to be celebrated, not squelched. I know it takes every ounce of patience you have to remember this when he acts out, weeps out, and shouts out, but try to remember that he is feeling every emotion exponentially. One father, at the end of his rope with a child who refused to fall asleep at night decided to write a poem to vent his frustration. *Go the F___ to Sleep* is the best-selling book that resulted from this nightly struggle. I'm sure you can relate!

I hope you can appreciate your energetic, enthusiastic (even for a little bit), curious (always), loyal, moral, creative (and all its messes), dramatic (drama queen), poetic, compassionate, empathetic, and self-aware child. I want you to revel in his great joy, and in her astonishment. I wish for you to acknowledge and relish the uniqueness of your overexciteable child and even……..you, because OE's are Great! Exciting! Fulfilling! Painful! Challenging! and Troublesome!

> *You are not accidental. Existence needs you. Without you, something will be missing in existence, and no one else can replace it.*
>
> *Osho, a Zen master*

CHAPTER **10**

Your Child Might Not Have ADHD (Attention Deficit with Hyperactivity Disorder)

Walk into any school nurse's office around lunch time and notice the small white medication containers lining the cabinet from one end to the other. Some children legitimately need medication for various illnesses, but many of those containers contain medication for ADHD. Three to seven percent of children, mostly boys (9:1) have this condition.

What if parents and teachers knew about another reason why certain children are restless, have little or no concentration, and jump from task to task? Let me give you some information that might cause you to take a second look at your child's behaviors.

This chapter will describe the overexciteabilities so you can see if any of them apply to your child, AND even to you. When I first learned about them, I was amazed that I have all five of them, some of them more intensely than others. Knowing about them certainly explained some of my own behaviors. It was an A-ha! Moment for me.

Let's see how you and your child do with them. First, I'll list them, then I'll explain them and give some examples.

Five Overexciteabilities

1. Psychomotor
2. Intellectual
3. Imaginational
4. Emotional
5. Sensual

Psychomotor overexciteability may be confused with ADHD. Youngsters with this quality have high degrees of energy, love, physical movement, are quite active, and strive to be in constant motion. You may have to tell them to slow down when they talk. Their need for intense physical activity seems insatiable. They are impulsive and seem restless much of the time. Does this describe anyone who lives at your house? If so, their teacher may think they are hyperactive and suggest they take medication for it.

Here's why you shouldn't do that: For certain children, intensity of physical activity is normal. Their bodies and minds cry out for it. This means you, as their parent, have a challenge. Still, having active, vital youngsters is better than having lethargic slugs, with you pushing and cajoling them to get up and do ANYTHING. Just do something.

Here are some ways to support a child with psychomotor OE: Encourage sports. When I go visit my grandson, Jack, age 11, I know our days will be filled with non-stop sports. First, we go out and shoot some hoops, then I teach him some drills to help develop his passing, defending, and dribbling. We have shooting contests, too. He has practiced so much it's a challenge to beat him.

Next, we play soccer. Again, I work with him on his dribbling, shooting, and passing. After that, we move on to volleyball. Then more instruction on serving and passing. Later, we get out the mitt, bat and softball. There's no instruction here, so we just play until we're tired of it.

◄ MOTHER AS EMOTIONAL COACH

Golf is next. Since this is one of my favorite sports, I hope he develops a love for it, so that in a few years, we can eliminate most of the other sports and just spend the day playing 18 holes, walking of course. Oh, yes, then it's time for either a walk or a bike ride, two other activities I hope he continues. i hope we can take a long bike adventure together when he is older. While we are walking or biking, we stop at the park to swing, play on the equipment, and climb on the rocks.

About this time, Jack's mother calls me on the cell phone, wondering where we are and what we're doing because it's almost time for dinner. Jack and I have spent the entire day playing and in motion, <u>loving every minute of it</u>. Reluctantly, we walk or ride home.

You might be getting tired just reading about all this activity, but that's an explanation of psychomotor overexciteability.

Summary:

Being in constant motion doesn't warrant an immediate diagnosis of ADHD and a prescription for medication.

Psychomotor overexciteability is a challenge, not a liability.

Be accepting of your child's need for physical activity and participate in sports or games that are fun for both of you.

Something to think about:

1. Remember back when you were a child. What were some of your favorite things to do? Given a day with no schedule, how did you fill that day? What about your spouse? Ask him these questions. This could spark an interesting conversation and you might find out some things about him you never knew before.

2. Go online to learn about ADHD. See how your child matches up with the characteristics given. Contrast these characteristics with the ones you now know about psychomotor overexciteability.

3. Buy or borrow books that tell about games or projects you and your child can play or do. Carve out time on your calendar for these activities.

CHAPTER 11

It's Your Fault The Kid's So Smart

It's all your fault, you know. If you and your spouse weren't so smart, the kid wouldn't be, either. As you read about OE's (overexciteabilities), you will probably see yourself again and again. Perhaps you will have empathy for what your daughter is going through, because you've been there yourself.

Just remember, the more OE's your child has and the more intense they are, the greater the potential for development. Perhaps you are asking yourself, "What if I don't want her to have so much potential? It's driving me crazy!" Well, then crazy you will go, because it's not going to go away. It's up to you to find a way to appreciate overexciteabilities.

Intellectual OE is pretty easy to discern; for example, if you are the parents of the eight-year-old girl who just qualified for the Scripps Spelling Bee and will be competing against boys and girls twice her age at the national level, it is obvious there's something unusual going on there. The girl's idea of fun is jumping on her trampoline while her mother gives her spelling words, the likes of which very few of us adults have even heard of, much less to be able to spell. Oh, and she's also interested in biology and ecology. She's already figured out what she wants to do with these interests when she gets old enough to stay away from home overnight by herself.

IT'S YOUR FAULT THE KID'S SO SMART

Then there is that reading thing. The spelling genius started reading when she was two years old. Rather unusual, don't you think? Of course, there are varying degrees of reading interest and ability. My grandson, Jack, whom I have mentioned in another chapter, seems to have quite a penchant for reading. A few years ago, our family was gathered at Lake Tahoe for a few days, some of those days snowbound, and I had an opportunity to observe his reading habits.

At age 7, after having gotten a good grasp on reading during the first semester of the second grade, the boy decided he wanted to read the Harry Potter series. This was no surprise to me, as I knew his father and mother had both devoured the series and the books were on the shelf at home. Immediately after Christmas, Jack began with the first volume, and by the middle of March, he was finishing up the last few pages of the last book. That's Intellectual OE!

If you have one child who has an OE or a collection of them…guess what? You might have a household of offspring like that. And you thought one was driving you crazy. That one is fanning the flame for the others.

Recently, I read in the paper about a high-school girl who had taken out a patent for a discovery she made that might help people with Alzheimer's Disease. I don't know about you, but it gives me hope for the future when I hear of someone this young who found her passion at an early age and who was fortunate enough to have parents and teachers who didn't pooh-pooh her ideas because of her age. Truly, these kids can show up at any age, in any grade, at anybody's household. What if one of them were sleeping under your roof? Would you hope she would forget about it, or are you prepared to go to any length to support her ideas?

But watch out for your child's welfare. Someone at your local school is going to notice this intensity, this passion, this extreme interest in a topic at an early age, and will try to tell you your child has Asperger's Syndrome. Some of the overexciteability characteristics may also look like Asperger's, so I hope you will be very careful before pinning a label on your child.

MOTHER AS EMOTIONAL COACH

Educate yourselves before making any decisions that might affect your child's future.

I wonder if you have a child who just loves flashlights and reading lamps attached to their headboard. It's no secret why they like these things. You and I used to love them, too, didn't we? We had a bedtime, but when mom or dad turned off the overhead light, we weren't finished reading. After burrowing under our sheets and blankets, we turned on our covert lights and read for hours until our eyes just couldn't stay awake any longer. We finished our book and fell asleep, satisfied with our completion. Morning came mighty early, but it was worth it.

Summary:

It's a good thing that your child exhibits Intellectual OE. It makes your life more interesting and fun, as you partner to satisfy her curiosity.

Keeping up with your child's intense interests can be a learning experience that gives you an opportunity to grow intellectually as well as to share what you know.

Even though the school may want to diagnose your child as having Asberger's Syndrome, pay attention to your own instincts and intuition.

Sometimes you have to turn your head the other way when you see a crack of light under your child's door late at night.

Something to think about:
1. Your intellectually overexciteable daughter might not be in the mainstream of interests for girls her age. Whenever she brings up a topic that you think is unusual, question her about it and together create ways to learn about the insects of Africa, for example. You'll both enjoy it.

2. Make sure she has friends who are intellectual peers. Plan outings that zero in on her interests. Invite friends over to discover the wonders of the heavens with a telescope, then have a sleepover in a tent, for example.

3. Just accept the fact that your child is not going to follow the crowd and doesn't care about most fads and activities that excite other kids. Make your own family's path, based on your child's interests. Everyone will derive inner satisfaction and delight.

CHAPTER **12**

They're Not Wasting Time Playing Legos

Caine Monroy is a 9-year-old boy living in East L.A. Last year, bored with being at his dad's used auto parts store every day with nothing to do, he decided to make a cardboard arcade. He gathered some tape, markers, plenty of large boxes and began his arcade by creating a soccer game. Next came a miniature basketball game, then his imagination went wild. He worked for months on his project, pretty soon covering the front of his dad's storefront with arcade games he invented and constructed.

When he was finished with the games, he sat day by day waiting for his first customer. It happened that his first customer came to the store to get a door handle for his car. When he saw Caine's Arcade, he was fascinated by the imaginative power of the young boy and asked if he could play a few games.

"Do you want a pass for $1.00 that lets you play four games, or do you want a $2.00 fun pass good for 15 plays?" Caine asked, thrilled to have a customer. What Caine did not know was that his first customer was a film-maker, Nirvan Millick. After playing a few games, he asked Caine's dad if he could make a short film about Caine's Arcade. Caine's father agreed, never anticipating that his son's creation was about to go viral.

Millick was not content to only post his film on Reddit. He also set up a website so viewers could contribute to Caine's college fund. In addition,

THEY'RE NOT WASTING TIME PLAYING LEGOS

he posted a surprise flash mob on Facebook. On the appointed day, hundreds of customers came to Caine's Arcade chanting, "We came to play!" And play they did—all day, in fact. Caine grinned for hours as he managed his busy cardboard arcade.

At the end of the day, he said, "Dad, this is the best day of my whole life."

His dad told reporters, "He doesn't watch much TV. He sits for hours and builds Legos."

Oh, and that college fund—over $239,000 so far.

Sooooooo—when your son or daughter spends endless hours captivated by their Legos, believe me, it's more than okay. Just remember Caine. He was creating without an audience. He had a dream, and the realization of his dream was much bigger than he ever could ever imagine. His success proves how the power of imagination resonates with so many people, regardless of their age.

Caine has imaginational overexciteabililty. His mind is constantly at work dreaming up new inventions, creative ideas, and he is never bored because he has his active mind to keep him company. He may also have imaginary friends and has probably read all of the Harry Potter books. Fantasy games are fun for him and you would be amazed at the detailed dreams he can recall.

When my children were youngsters, my mother-in-law would bring piles of computer print-outs from her workplace and give them to our kids. They were thrilled. They didn't care about all the numbers on one side of the paper. All they knew was that on the other side, they had hundreds of feet of paper to draw on, to create cartoons on, to stamp on, and could go wherever their imaginations led them with these reams of endless possibilities. Every once in awhile, I run across some of that fabulous display of creativity, and I love to think back on those wonderful childhood memories.

◄ MOTHER AS EMOTIONAL COACH

Your kids do this. They are jam-packed full of imagination and love to spend hours exploring their thoughts and feelings in the world of science, technology, engineering, art, and mathematics. These activities are stepping-stones for their emotional development, and you are supplying them with the time and materials for their exploration. Never mind that you can seldom find a marker or pen where you left it and your house looks like the city depository for recycled paper. They have something they need to draw or something they need to build and they don't have time to be neat and orderly about it! Let the little urchins have at it!!

Just remember, OE's came as original equipment with your child. There's not much you can do to get rid of them. So, you'd might as well resign yourself to a life of constant activity and tune up your own imagination so you can play with them and enjoy it. Another word that you might relate to is superstimulability. So, you have your choice of two multiple-syllabic words to throw around, perhaps to your pediatrician or to your child's teacher.

Your child's teacher will love your child's imagination. This will be the child in the class who writes the play, plays the lead role, paints the scenery, and makes their own costume! This is the student who has zero tolerance for boredom, so hope that he gets a teacher who is project-oriented and loves lots of action in the classroom.

On the other hand, if you draw a teacher who wants everyone sitting with their hands folded listening for directions on the next task, then you have trouble and the school year is going to get really long. Perhaps you could schedule a meeting with him and offer some suggestions about some ways in which he can keep your child engaged. Yes, engaged is the key word. Your child will have a challenge to keep engaged with paper-and-pencil activities, but will be a breeze to work with if given opportunities to learn creatively, such as making a mural illustrating the main points of a book he has read.

THEY'RE NOT WASTING TIME PLAYING LEGOS

There's a downside to having an active imagination. Your child can be annoying and irritable to others who are not so exciteable. One of those most-annoyed people could be his own teacher. You have your work cut out for you in helping your child realize that his imagination could be rubbing his teacher and classmates the wrong way. He is one of many vying for attention and he must learn to take his turn. Others have good ideas, too, and he must not dominate conversations or brainstorming sessions. It doesn't matter how great his ideas are if he is interrupting others to share them.

I'm going to throw something in here that might be controversial, but I believe kids with high intensity and its resulting anxiety can calm themselves by doing yoga. Some people think yoga is some voodoo kind of quirky religion and certainly don't want it happening at school, although some schools are doing it. Any of you who have done yoga feel its results in your own life, and I think you can do you and your child a favor by introducing it at home.

My eight-year-old intense grandson practices yoga with his aunt. He loves doing it alongside her and even though he doesn't know what it's doing for him, I can see what a calming effect it has on him.

You are lucky that your child has a vivid imagination. It makes life more colorful for him and for your whole family. Just remember that when he is moving his hands quickly to reach for the next important part for his Lego creation, this is a good thing. It's far from wasting time. He may be imagining the next technological or engineering creation that will enhance all of our lives.

One Christmas, I asked our fifteen-year-old son, Trent, what he wanted for a gift.

"You're not going to believe this, Mom, but I want some Legos. I thought I had outgrown them, but I guess I haven't."

He got his Legos. And I got the job of sweeping them out of the carpet, just like I did back when he was seven.

◄ MOTHER AS EMOTIONAL COACH

Play is the work of a child. While they are playing, they are imagining a world of their own making. Support this play by encouraging, asking questions, and even getting down on the floor and creating an object of your own imagination. Those piles of laundry will wait. You can mow the yard tomorrow. Your child's imagination needs your back right now.

If you keep enough markers and paper available, this is much of what your child's active imagination needs. They don't need expensive supplies from an art store. Let them pay for that themselves when they are grown and have an income of their own. For right now, keep it simple.

Help your child develop social skills to accompany his other talents. He will be happier than if others must endure his constant intensity and his engine running in high gear. Teach him how to settle himself and to respect others' ideas.

Summary:
Leave your child alone long enough and you will be surprised by what he will create.

Teach your child to respect not only her own ideas, but also the ideas of others. They can learn to listen to one another's unique thoughts and appreciate them.

You might enjoy taking part in some of your child's creative adventures. Make time for it. Make sure you're invited to participate, however.

Something to think about:
1. It was your lucky day when your child with an overexcitable imagination was born. You will never be bored. You may wear yourself

THEY'RE NOT WASTING TIME PLAYING LEGOS

out making sure that this imagination has materials to play with and to create with, but you will not have to entertain this child. His mind is going like a turbine engine, full speed ahead. Just sit back and enjoy watching this wondrous human being. It's children like this who grow up and change our world.

2. When you walk into your child's room and almost faint from the chaos you see, just back straight out and close the door behind you. This child will always be messy. His desk at school will be a mess; his closet is a jumble; the floor is strewn with things he was really interested in right before he became intensely interested in a new idea and its inherent mess. You just have to increase your propensity for dealing with it, or just never go into his room. That's one of the jobs of a parent with this overexcitability.

3. Some people, usually his relatives, will dub him "the absent-minded professor." Yes, they will notice his imagination, distractedness, messiness, the shirt on backwards. Just brush this off, and continue supporting his off-the-beaten-path way of being. Face it—he's never going to be in the normal category. Make that okay with you.

CHAPTER **13**

Secrets of a Drama Queen (and Why Being One is a Good Thing)

Society has made light of people, both male and female, who have intense feelings, both in themselves and for others. We are surprised when we see our House Majority Leader tearing up, unable to speak or go on. We are mystified when we watch our sports figures get emotional and cry on camera, like Tony Gonzalez did when the Atlanta Falcons won their way to the NFL playoffs. Barack Obama shed tears on nation wide TV while comforting the nation about the Sandy Hook tragedy.

We are not surprised when we see the parade of women Oscar winners crying as they accept their statuette. It isn't unusual at all to watch Robin Roberts' fellow *Today Show* hosts cry along with her as she announces her bone marrow transplant news. It's a societal norm for women to cry, even in public; not so for men.

What all of these public figures have in common is Emotional Overexcitability (Emotional OE). It is both a blessing and a burden. Noone wants to be labeled a Drama Queen, because the term implies acting out a role for effect. In actuality, emotional overexciteabililty is real life to individuals who experience it. It may seem like they are trying to attract attention to themselves and we may get sick and tired of their cry-baby ways, but their emotional intensity is the norm for them.

Not only that, children with high OE are also extreme at the other end of the spectrum—such as happiness, excitedness, euphoria, and optimism. Your child will relate to another child's emotional state because she has a radar-like sense of empathy. Watch out when choosing movies to watch, for example, because she *becomes* that actor, feels those feelings, and reacts to it emotionally. Same goes for books she reads or DVD's she watches.

As she plays, her emotions are interwoven into what she is doing. To her, playing is *real*. She has a wide emotional spectrum and calls upon it to enhance her sense of adventure, invention, and imagination. She will probably have imaginary friends, which is good. They might keep her occupied while you get caught up on your e-mail.

I know you have been told it's okay for your children to see your emotions, such as crying when you are upset and telling her you really are okay and you'll be over it in a few minutes. Save your big crying jags for your own private place, though, because your emotionally overexcitable daughter is extremely tuned into your emotions, and won't leave your side until she knows you're back to normal.

Children with emotional OE also pick up on relationship issues between parents. You don't have to scream and yell at one another in front of them. Somehow, their emotional radar can burn through walls of your house when you think you are alone while discussing a highly-charged topic. When you return to the family and pretend everything is back to normal when you know it isn't, they know, too. Not wanting to let you know they know, they internalize it. This is not good for emotional development. In fact, it impedes it. It's like a highway strewn with garbage as they try to navigate their life's path.

Your child has enough to deal with emotionally concerning their own issues. They don't need yours getting in their way. They are not equipped to deal with your problems, so don't let your problems become their problems,

MOTHER AS EMOTIONAL COACH

because it will come out all wrong for them. Their information is sketchy; their solutions are immature; they become confused and emotionally disoriented in their own home. You don't want this to happen to your child. Solve your own problems so you can help them solve theirs. Persistent and chronic issues such as alcoholism, infidelity, substance abuse, and parental absence in the home guarantees a messed-up kid. Look around you in the neighborhood. You'll see what I mean.

Dabrowski wrote that emotional development is the most important of all the ways we develop. You might think that intellectual development is the most important. Don't believe them. You've probably noticed the seminars and workshops you can attend and magazine articles you can read that help you discover your E.Q. and then teach you ten things you can do to enhance it. This isn't just for kids. You need to know your capacity for emotional development. Being aware of your feelings, the feelings of others, finding out the cause of these feelings, and knowing the likely effect of your feelings on others will provide your child with an emotional role model. And boy, does this take a lot of time!

You can't sweep feelings under the carpet and pretend they went away. Not only do they not go away, they linger and affect every other aspect of your being. I call it "burning the rug" when parents take time to unearth those hidden feelings, both in themselves and in their child. There's nowhere to hide feelings when you make the commitment to address emotional issues within a short period of time from when they happened.

You might feel reluctant to bring up an issue you know will cause pain or other negative emotions. You might want to pretend certain events never happened. It takes a courageous parent to face a child's unresolved negative emotions, especially if that parent caused those emotions. Noone wants to see their child hurting. If you're like me, I'd rather hurt than see my child hurt. But their feelings have not gone away; they are still causing pain for your child, even though it is not apparent. Buck up, take a deep breath, and plunge into a conversation about these unresolved, but important parts of your child's psyche. Rinse out that container called psyche daily, because when tomorrow comes, there will be something new to fill it.

Here's what happens if you don't take this emotional responsibility: Feelings live with us. You grow up. You get married. You face problems, but guess what? You were never taught how to resolve your negative feelings, so here they are 30 years later. You make an appointment with a psychologist or marriage counselor. You struggle to deal with the feelings, issues, and incidents of your past. It's expensive. You are embarrassed that you can't solve your problems by yourself. You realize you have to face it now or face it later.

Spending part of your time as a parent dealing your child's feelings is time well-spent. On one recent trip to California to see my grandchildren, John and I were sitting at the table with my highly emotional 8-year-old grandson, Aaron. Aaron looked at John and asked, "When is the last time you cried?" John, a little taken aback by the question, but not hesitating, replied, "I guess it was about three and a half years ago when my wife died. I cried quite a bit." Aaron said, "Oh." John told me later he decided to tell the truth instead of trying to hide behind a tough-guy persona and say he didn't ever cry.

If you have a child like Aaron, please take time to answer these all-important questions. Please don't brush them aside or tell them they're silly for asking. Make room in your life for these precious interactions with your emotionally overexcited child. It's a gift, both for your child and for yourself.

Summary:

Boys and girls who are emotionally overexciteable have the best and the worst of both worlds. On one hand, it is marvelous to have such a rich emotional life. They don't miss a nuance. They pick up on everything going on around them, as well as what is going on within themselves.

MOTHER AS EMOTIONAL COACH

On the other hand, being emotionally aware is a burden, especially for boys. Although it is becoming more and more acceptable to put one's emotions out on public display, it still is not the norm. It is your job as a parent to support their emotional life, knowing that is one of the greatest gifts they could have been born with.

As a parent, it is your obligation to work out your own emotions in a healthy manner, and a manner that doesn't leave debris for your child to pick up and have to live with. Her own wastebasket is enough to take out every day, much less having to carry your adult issues to the curb. Don't put this burden on your child.

Fearlessly and courageously, do whatever it takes to clear up what is impeding your progress toward emotional stability. Look at the nightly news and you will see countless examples of people who are using their child as a dumping ground for what's wrong with themselves. Don't let your child get caught in the crossfire of your problems.

Something to think about:

1. Your moments of joy are plentiful if your child is emotionally overexcitable. You get to experience her highs and lows on a daily basis. Watch as she gets attached to people and to animals, then all of a sudden feels lonely. Be thankful you get to ride along in her roller-coaster life. Be glad. Be compassionate like she is. Cry together. Laugh together. Don't take any of the bad stuff personally. Understand that her moods and sensitivities are gifts to you, to your family, and to the world.

2. And here's something hopeful for her future: Daniel Goleman, author of *Emotional Intelligence*, said recently in an interview that to be in a top profession, aside from having an IQ one standard deviation from the mean (the mean being 100), a person needs the ability to be self-motivated and emotionally intelligent. He added that emotional intelligence is one of the many intelligences that everyone has. You go, girl!

CHAPTER **14**

Where's My Blankie?

I wonder if your son has a blankie, some worthless (to you), moth-eaten piece of fabric that was so cute when he was born, but now that he is seven, it seems ridiculous. He has to take it to bed each night and won't go to sleep or anywhere else without it. You sneak into his room at night and ever so carefully unloosen the blankie from his grip so you can wash it and replace it before morning. That's right after you gingerly take your sleeping daughter's tattered and torn hippopotamus from her arms so you can wash it in the same load.

This same daughter might be unable to stand anything tight around her waist nor will she wear anything scratchy, like those net tu-tu's, given to her by both grandmothers who thought she would look oh-so-cute in them, yet they languish in the drawer.

Then there may be a boy in your house who only eats chicken nuggets because he doesn't like the smell of vegetables or fruit. In fact, he can't stand the smell of frying hamburgers or boiling spaghetti, either. And a dozen other things.

All of these kids were born with original equipment called Sensual Overexciteability. You may receive a phone call from school requesting a meeting, and at that meeting, you discover they want to diagnose your child as having sensory integration disorder (SID). Do your homework and

MOTHER AS EMOTIONAL COACH

educate yourself about this before agreeing to label your child. For one thing, this label will follow him all the way through school. Be cautious about doing this.

When you get back home and start to think about it, you probably realize how tired you are of listening to his constant complaints about the air conditioner being too loud, the music being too noisy, or the ice clinking in the glass. And, don't even think about setting off loud fireworks around him unless you want to endure some strong negative reactions. You probably knew about his dislike of loud noises from when he was a baby, just like you knew he didn't want a wet diaper on. He let you know immediately when it was time to get rid of that thing. He's always going to be sensitive to sound and touch.

I must have some of this Sensual OE myself. It really bugs me when I am in a writing class and I hear the scraping noise of pen on paper or hear the faint sound of keyboards being tapped near me.

There are lots of good points to being Sensually Overexciteable. You've probably noticed your son lingering over a little bug he sees marching across the lawn. He will probably spend several minutes looking at it and watching its movement. Your daughter may run into the house at dusk wanting you to come outside and look at the awesome sunset. Your children might love camping, where they can see, hear, and smell the out-of-doors. Spending time at an art gallery or sculpture museum is a delight, and his favorite class is art, where he can work with various shapes, textures, and colors, creating to his heart's delight.

One day last spring, John and I took Sarah, my 5-year-old granddaughter, on a train ride from Folsom, California, to downtown Sacramento. When we arrived at our destination, we walked a couple of blocks to a park in the middle of the city. In the park was a sculpture garden honoring our military men and women. They weren't stiff statues on stands, but bronze sculptures of men and women in natural poses. Sarah zeroed in on one particular sculpture of a seated soldier cradling his weapon.

I think that little girl put her hand on every square inch of that soldier and spent a long time doing it. I wandered among the sculptures, keeping my eye on her. She seemed entranced by the feel of the bronze. I also heard her talking to him. She was mesmerized.

Other activities for children with sensual OE's could be attending concerts, as well as listening to music at home. Even at a very early age, children with sensual overexciteability love to squeeze clay or play-doh between their fingers. Your son may have a favorite guitarist who plays music that inspires his artistic talent. Provide artist's dates for him, where you play his favorite music while the two of you paint or draw. Don't forget to display his masterpieces! Children with Sensual OE love being the center of attention and this is one way to do it. You might also notice their excessive sociability, their inability to tolerate being alone, and their ability to derive comfort from over-eating.

More than likely, sensual OE combines with other OE's in your child, such as imaginational, intellectual, or emotional. Sensual OE merely enhances and intensifies the other OE's in this case. As if your household needs more enhancement or intensity! If so, rejoice in all that is happening around you. Be glad you were given the privilege to observe and guide all of this excitement and talent. Not everyone could do it, but you can, because you remember yourself at her age, full of life, overflowing with ideas, living in a rich and intense world every day of your life.

You couldn't wait for tomorrow to come because you had so much to do, multitudes of things to make, so many kids to have fun with, and a myriad of ideas for inventions, clubs, and sports. Life was an exciting event. I hope you will provide the living space for your child to have a glorious childhood.

◄ MOTHER AS EMOTIONAL COACH

Your child with Sensual Overexciteability might drive you nuts at times. He is ever aware of touch, smell, taste, and sound without really trying. He is highly sensitive in these ways.

He likes to be affectionate. He needs to touch and be touched. He likes to be hugged and kissed. This is him. This is who he is. If he is not validated in his sensual needs, he may feel deprived and find other ways and places to get his needs met.

He may lack the ability for reflection, planning, and systematic effort. This may be interpreted at school as a student who doesn't care or who may be a candidate for a label of ADHD.

We've already talked about that, so again I say, please avoid labeling your child at all costs. That might sound dramatic, but it is very important not to slot your child into a place where he might not belong.

A child with Sensual Overexciteability may appear to be living in his own world and might seem to have little interest in the lives of others. You might notice his superficial attitude about loss and death. He may have a tendency to externalize problems and to blame others. These characteristics are just a part of the package with children who have Sensual OE, and must be respected and supported.

Hold your tongue. Do not judge him. This boy has a different way of looking at the world, especially in combination with Emotional, Imaginational, and Intellectual Overexciteability. Go along with him and his interests. It will probably be a fun journey!

Summary:

You will pick right up on a child who has sensual overexcitability. They take up alot of your time.

The sensually overexcitable child will surprise you again and again when she notices things that no one else does.

Practice your patience with the sensually overexcitable child. He stops and smells the roses alot.

WHERE'S MY BLANKIE?

Something to think about:

1. You have a unique individual on your hands. Watching a sunset together, marveling at a lion in the zoo, standing for ten minutes in front of a large mural—these moments take a lot of your time. But, it's worth it. You are relationship-building with your child. You might not even like doing any of these things and you really don't have to like them. All you have to do is appreciate your child's interests. Who knows, you may learn to stop and smell the roses with him.

2. You can encourage her to do things that bring her pleasure. You can compliment her for being definitive about what she likes and doesn't like. She might enjoy being nudged in a different direction than she usually goes, in regard to trying new things and exploring new experiences. When you're about to pull your hair out about her picky eating, gently and in a fun way, challenge her try something different. Applaud her awareness of sights, sounds and textures that others miss.

3. If it is possible at your house, allow her to have her own room. Let her select her own color(s) for the walls and choose the comforter for her bed. Make sure she has plenty of display space for all of her artwork and souvenirs. This will be her own kingdom and she can play, play away. Please don't stifle her creativity with electronics in her private kingdom. Place these in a common family area where she can be with family members as she watches her favorite shows or plays her favorite video games.

4. For a parent who is active and constantly on-the-go, having a child who lives basically in the here-and-now is a living lesson sitting right there in your hearth room. You, too, can take time to enjoy today. You might like the difference it makes in the mood and attitude of your family.

Conclusion: You ARE an Emotional Coach

Somewhere in the middle of my parenting years, when the kids were around eight to ten years old, I finally figured it out. Up to that point, I was busy packing lunches, washing clothes, coordinating sports, Scouts, school, and church schedules, buying birthday gifts, and cooking meals. I didn't really have time to think much about myself, other than being a mom. You know how endless that job is.

What I finally figured out was that this parenting job was much more than the physical part of taking care of my children, although without me doing those things, our home would have been a mad-house. Even more important than keeping their toilets clean and their clothes washed and put away, my main job was being their emotional coach.

It's really easy to see when the carpet needs sweeping or the dishwasher needs unloading, but a child's emotional needs are not quite that obvious. They don't always recognize their emotions. They know they feel something but do not have the maturity to analyze what it is and to respond to it in an appropriate manner.

That's where you come in. You are your child's only mother. You are the closest one to observe the nuances that only a mother could notice. Your emotional radar needs to be on high alert at all times. You need to monitor what is going on with your child's emotional status on a daily basis.

YOU ARE AN EMOTIONAL COACH

It would be easier to function as a housekeeper, merely looking after your child's possessions, making sure they have something to eat, and observing a bed-time. But that makes you a machine, and you are far from that. You must be tuned in to their moods.

You must know what situations are joyful for them and which ones make them feel sad.

Being a sensitive kid is not easy. Not only do they feel their own emotions, they actually feel what others feel. Your home needs to provide an environment that understands their emotional intensity. Don't neglect or negate their feelings. Accept them, discuss them, give them a sense of importance. You need to be emotionally alive yourself. It should be okay to cry in your home.

Never allow feelings to be buried. This stunts them emotionally and has repercussions for the future when they are unable to form deep, intimate relationships. You've seen men who act out the pain they feel from being undeveloped emotionally. Even though there are lots of jokes about these guys, having a warped personality rears its ugly head at the most inopportune moments and causes pain for other family members.

Let their personalities develop naturally as they grow up in your home. Perhaps they will end up helping others whose mothers did not have the privilege of knowing what you have learned about what it takes to raise an emotionally well-adjusted child.

You are the one who helps them develop trust, trust that someone will always have their back, no matter what. You are that special someone.

In this book, I have explained some things that are essential for you to know about how to effectively parent your child. On the next few pages, you will find Kamierz Dabrowski's Theory of Positive Disintegration (The Theory of Emotional Development). It tells in more detail what I have already told you. It will help you to understand yourself better, which in turn will enable you to be alert to your child's developmental stages.

◀ **MOTHER AS EMOTIONAL COACH**

Later on, when you have grandchildren, like me, you can have the joy of observing their children's development. They will appreciate your ability to be someone other than the one who brings them toys. It will make them happy to know there is a older someone who understands them and what they are all about.

On the following pages, there are some resources for you if you wish to do further reading on the subject. I hope you have shared the ideas in this book with your friends and with your spouse. Perhaps you have had a discussion group and have grown as a parent and as a person as a result of your participation. Always remember: It's worth it!!

On my recent birthday, my daughter gave me a decorative box sign that says: "If I didn't have you as a mom, I'd choose you as a friend." That's worth a million dollars to me. It indeed was worth it.

Appendix I: The Theory of Positive Disintegration

I mentioned earlier in the preface that my colleague, Karen Nelson, wrote an article in Linda Silverman's *Advanced Development Journal (January 1989)* about Dabrowski's Theory of Positive Development. The following explanation of the theory is quoted directly from that article.

Dabrowski's Theory of Positive Disintegration

Piagetian developmental theorists have emphasized cognitive development, with little attention to the role of emotions in development. Dabrowski's Theory of Positive Development (TPD) stresses the **affective** aspect of development. It attempts to explain, not just describe, developmental transformations as a sequence of five levels. Each level constitutes a distinct personality structure or behavioral organization. The emotional forces that distinguish the levels are called *dynamisms* to indicate their dynamic potency to promote development. Developmental potential is the underlying principle that provides continuity between the levels. Each level represents an advancement over the previous level. Transformation is from simple to complex, from the most automatic to the most voluntary (Piechowski, 1975).

Dabrowski observed that the most gifted and creative individuals with whom he worked seemed to exhibit higher levels of empathy, sensitivity, moral responsibility, self-reflection, and autonomy of thought than the general population. During times of crisis, these same individuals exhibited so-called neurotic symptoms—intense inner conflict, feelings of inferiority toward their own ideals, feelings of inadequacy, shame and guilt, and existential anxiety and despair.

Dabrowski suggested that such individuals were "positively maladjusted." They had evolved beyond the societal norm and experienced great pain in the awareness of their differences from the norm. Because of the suffering and distress that accompanied growth or developmental transformation, Dabrowski called it *positive disintegration*—a process whereby simpler and less mature psychological structures composing the personality break down in order for more complex and advanced structures to rise.

Dabrowski not only observed that the inner conflict generated by the disintegration process was necessary for attaining higher levels of human functioning, but he also concluded that most persons do not attain these higher levels. Most people are egocentric and unprincipled, or they are crowd followers, lacking an integrated set of inner values.

Dabrowski postulated five qualitatively different kinds of human development, each with a distinguishable personality organization.

Level I: Primary Integration

At Level I, *Primary Integration,* egocentrism prevails. A person at this level lacks the capacity for empathy and self-examination. When things go wrong, someone else is always to blame; self-responsibility is not a Level I characteristic. With nothing within to inhibit personal ambition, Level I individuals often attain power in society by ruthless means. An example might be an arms dealer, who will promote war for the sake of the millions of dollars of profit to be gained. Never is the question of the resulting death and destruction an issue to be considered—personal gain is primary. There appears to be no anguish over the conflict between greed

APPENDIX I: THE THEORY OF POSITIVE DISINTEGRATION

and the less tangible value of human life. Dabrowski observed that political and social leaders often come from this developmental stratum.

Level II: Unilevel Disintegration

Level II individuals are influenced primarily by their social group and by mainstream values, or they are moral relativists for whom "anything goes," morally speaking. They often exhibit ambivalent feelings and indecisive behavior because they have no clear cut set of self-determined internal values. At Level II, which Dabrowski called *Unilevel Disintegration*, inner conflict is horizontal, a competition between equal, competing values.

Tolstoy's Anna Karenina is an example of Unilevel Disintegration. She cannot sort out for herself a hierarchy of values that distinguishes "what is" from "what ought to be." Her situation is tragically difficult, but she seems to lack the inner resources (or developmental potential) for the task.

Level III: Spontaneous Multilevel Disintegration

At Level III, *multilevelness* arises. The person develops a hierarchical sense of values. Inner conflict is vertical, a struggle to bring one's behavior up to higher standards. There is a dissatisfaction with what one is, because of competing sense of what one could and ought to be, the personality ideal. This internal struggle between higher and lower can be accompanied by existential despair, anxiety, depression, and feelings of dissatisfaction with the self.

Traditional psychologies often interpret the affect exhibited at Level III as symptomatic of psychoneurosis that must be "cured" so the individual can lead a "normal" life. Dabrowski disagreed. He insisted that psychoneurosis is not an illness. If there are neurotic symptoms, they can be signs of *positive disintegration* whereby simpler, more instinctual psychological structures are being replaced by more complex and conscious structures. Personality ideal is arising; personality is evolving in the direction of the ideal.

Whereas individuals at Level II are content with mainstream values of the family, church, and society, at Level III one senses, *No one else is going to tell me what truth is, what life means. No one can tell me what my life means. Is there a God? Am I here for a purpose? What purpose?*

The Level III personality does not idly contemplate these questions as abstract issues. He or she feels them in the soul. Not knowing answers can be anguish. When the soul finds its answers, they compel response from life. Dabrowski and Piechowski (1977) consider Dostoyevski's *Crime and Punishment* a demonstration of the Level III conflict between higher and lower values. Tolstoy also expressed his own multilevel conflicts in his compelling novels.

Heredity and environment govern Levels I and II, but for Level III development to be possible, a person must be able to assert self-awareness, self-direction, and self-discipline to overcome genetic propensities, upbringing, and external circumstance. The *autonomous factor* is a will to grow through inner psychic transformation. A sense of responsibility—not only for one's actions but also for one's development—characterizes advanced development.

The *autonomous factor* is a powerful force propelling development toward higher levels of integrity and authenticity. Level III individuals can envision what they would like to be, but they do not yet hold the means of meeting their own ideals.

Level IV: Organized Multilevel Disintegration

In comparison to Level III, which he called *Spontaneous Multilevel Disintegration* (the level of emotional tumult), Dabrowski called Level IV, *Organized Multlilevel Disintegration*. Level IV individuals are well on the road to self-actualization. They have found a way to meet their own ideals, and they are effective leaders in society. They show high levels of responsibility, authenticity, reflective judgment, empathy for others, autonomy of thought and action, self-awareness, and other attributes associated with self-actualization.

Piechowski (1986) concluded that Eleanor Roosevelt is an example of at least Level IV development. Her life is an example of self-actualization. The extent and power of her compassion, and the deliberate effort to follow Christ as her inner ideal, reveal characteristics in her development that go even higher, from Level IV to Level V.

From early childhood, Eleanor Roosevelt exerted her will to conquer tears, fatigue, her voice, physical awkwardness, numerous fears, ingrained social and racial prejudice, depressions, and loss of love. In all this, her life of prayer was hidden, but the work of inner psychic transformation was always there (Piechowski, 1986).

The first half of her life was her struggle for self-mastery. Later, her principal goal was the service to her country and the whole world.

Level V Secondary Integration

At Level V, the struggle for self-mastery has been won. Inner conflicts regarding the self have been resolved through actualization of the personality ideal. Disintegration has been transcended by the integration of one's values and ideals into one's living and being. Life is lived in service to humanity. It is lived according to the highest, most universal principles of loving, compassionate regard for the worth of the human individual. Dabrowski called this the level of *Secondary Disintegration*.

As an example, think of the life of Mother Teresa. Self-concerns are transcended. Her love for the poor makes them equal, however widely they differ in intellectual and other attainments.

Appendix II: Developmental Potential

Dabrowski found that five types of "increased psychic excitability" were predictive of developmental potential. He called these *overexcitabilities* (OE's). They are assumed to be part of a person's constitution and to be more or less independent of each other.

Psychomotor overexcitability is expressed as high degrees of energy, activity, and movement. It manifests as love of movement, rapid speech, pursuit of intense physical activity, pressure for action, impulsiveness, and restlessness.

Sensual overexcitability involves an intensity and craving for pleasure, a "keen sensual aliveness" (Piechowski 1986) to sights, smells, tastes, textures, and sounds. Sensual OE can be expressed in seeking sensual outlets for inner tensions, especially through overeating and varieties of sexual experience.

Intellectual overexcitability includes questioning, questing, analysis, problem-solving, theoretical thinking, and the capacity for sustained intellectual effort. It is not synonymous with intelligence, because many intelligent individuals do not derive great pleasure from intellectual pursuits.

Imaginational overexcitability is vivid imagery, invention, and the capacity for creative imagination. It can be recognized through rich association of images and impressions, animated visualization, use of image and metaphor in verbal expression, predilection for fantasy, and ability to tell dreams in vivid detail.

APPENDIX II: DEVELOPMENTAL POTENTIAL

Manifestations of *emotional overexcitability* include intensity of feeling, inhibition, strong affective memory, concern with death, anxieties, fears, guilt, depression and suicidal moods. Most notable of the emotional OE's are relationship feelings; rich differentiated interpersonal feeling "is the mainstuff of individual development from a lower to a higher level" (Piechowski, 1979).

Emotional OE, usually in combination with heightened intellectual OE, is the most significant of the OE's for indicating strong potential for advanced development.

Appendix III:
A Poem by Kazimierz Dabrowski

Hail to you, psychoneurotics,
   For you perceive sensibility
        in the insensibility of the world,
  uncertainty in its certainty.
           For you are often as conscious of others
              as of yourself,
           For you feel the anxiety of the world,
                      its limits and its false unlimited assurance...

           For your fear of the absurdity of existence,
...For your awkwardness
        for your transcendental realism
          and your lack of daily realism...
     For your creativity and your ecstasy,
   For your maladjustment to what is
            and your adjustment to what ought to be,
       For your immense possibilities not yet actualized...

                For what is unique, original, intuitive and
infinite in you.
        For the solitude and the oddness of your paths.

            Hail to you.

Bibliography

Ackerman, C. (2009). The essential elements of Dabrowski's theory of positive disintegration and how they are connected. Retrieved 2/8/2013 from thefreelibrary.com.

Bradberry, T. & Greaves, J. (2009). *Emotional Intelligence 2.0*. San Diego: Talent Smart.

Cornwell, S. (2009). *The Emotional Curriculum: A Journey Towards Emotional Literacy*. New York: Lucky Duck.

Goleman, D. (1995). *Emotional Intelligence: Why it can matter more than IQ*. New York: Bantam.

Goleman, D. (1998). *Working with Emotional Intelligence*. New York: Bantam.

Gottman, J. (1997). *Raising an Emotionally Intelligent Child*. New York: Fireside.

Jacobsen, M. (1999). *The Gifted Adult: A Revolutionary Guide for Liberating Everyday Genius*. New York: Random House.

Jawer, M. & Micozzi, M. (2009). *The Spiritual Anatomy of Emotion*. Rochester, VT: Park Street.

Lantieri, L. (2008). *Building Emotional Intelligence*. Boulder, CO: Sounds True.

LeDoux, J. (1996). *The Emotional Brain*. New York: Touchstone.

McLaren, K. (2001). *Emotional Genius*. Columbia, CA: Laughing Tree.

Piechowski, M. & Daniels, S., Eds. (2009). *Living With Intensity*. Scottsdale: Great Potential.

Ryback, D. (1998). *Putting Emotional Intelligence to Work*. Woburn, MA: Butterworth-Heinemann.

Salovey, P. & Sluyter, D. (1997). *Emotional Development and Emotional Intelligence*. New York: Basic.

Segal, J. (1997). *Raising Your Emotional Intelligence*. New York: Holt

Segall, J. (2008). *The Language of Emotional Intelligence*. New York: McGraw-Hill.

Silverman, L. (2013). *Giftedness 101*. New York: Springer.

Silverman, L. (2009). My love affair with Dabrowski's theory: a personal odyssey. Retrieved 2/8/13 from thefreelibrary.com

Simmons, S. & Simmons, J. (1997). *Measuring Emotional Intelligence*. Arlington, TX: Summit.

Spendlove, D. (2009). *Emotional Literacy: Ideas in Action*. New York: Lucky Duck .

Steiner, C. (1997). *Achieving Emotional Literary*. New York: Avon.

Walker, S. (2002). *The Survival Guide for Parents of Gifted Kids*. Minneapolis: Free Spirit.

To order copies of this book: stephanyhughes.com

To read more by this author: hippospeaks.blogspot.com

To contact the author: stephippo@aol.com